THE POWER OF YOUR SMILE

Dr. William J. Kalanta

WESTBOW
PRESS®
A DIVISION OF THOMAS NELSON
& ZONDERVAN

WestBow Press books may be ordered through booksellers or by contacting:

WestBow Press
A Division of Thomas Nelson & Zondervan
1663 Liberty Drive
Bloomington, IN 47403
www.westbowpress.com
844-714-3454

ISBN: 978-1-6642-8554-5 (sc)
ISBN: 978-1-6642-8556-9 (hc)
ISBN: 978-1-6642-8555-2 (e)

Library of Congress Control Number: 2022922231

Print information available on the last page.

WestBow Press rev. date: 01/18/2023

Notebook 1

Make a note to smile.

I don't know why things happen. One day, I was sitting at my kitchen counter writing jokes for my latest comedy book. I was penning many varieties of jokes covering numerous topics. Suddenly, I wrote a funny joke about the human smile. I don't know why, but my mind started overflowing with clever sayings, idioms, sage advice, witticisms, jokes, and many new views and opinions concerning the human smile. Over the course of the next forty-eight hours, I pretty much sat at my kitchen counter and wrote all of my thoughts about a smile as fast as I could, and then I slept for twelve hours. Upon awakening, I realized I had crafted the beginnings of a great book.

The culmination of those thoughts and many nights of editing resulted in this book, which contains thousands of thoughts to ponder concerning such a simple action as a human smile. I don't know why I got off track and focused on this one simple instinctive concept: smiling.

I feel it was due to this COVID era. A major change was now required: wearing face masks when interacting with other humans. You don't miss something until it's gone. The face mask removed our smiles from being seen by others. I missed seeing them. Was she really smiling at me under that mask? It was like only seeing part of the picture and I didn't like it. It made me realize more than ever that smiles plays an important role in our lives. Scientific evidence even proves that smiling is good for the heart and blood pressure as well as one's psychological and social well-being. People are always looking for happiness. New research reveals, the act of smiling leads to chemical changes that make us feel happy.

A smile is a graceful curve that God put on our faces to remind us of how gracious He is and how grateful we are.

I smile contentedly, knowing my book has no table of contents.

A smile is how you show your mom you're thankful she made your favorite macaroni and cheese.

God gave us smiles and His saving grace as a simple way for us to save face.

A smile can also be found in a zip-up lip-locker version for easy storage and easy access for later.

A smile is an unzipper of your lips and the nicest way to zip your lips.

A smile planted on your face makes everything it's planted on still have plenty of space.

No matter how many smiles I receive, my face will always have plenty of room for mine.

I have a classic, sporty, quick, priceless smile parked out front in the space on my face called my lips.

My smile is not for sale; it can't be bought, only fraught. It can't be leased, only released. It can't be financed because it has nothing to put down.

Q: When was the last time you smiled?
A: I dunno, but I do know it was a long smile back or maybe it was just a smile ago.

A smile is a gesture way of helping.

A smile is your face's self-service line. A smile is your face's express line. Anyway, it's definitely some kind of a checkout line because a smile says, "Hey, check me out."

A smile can go on for smile-ions of smiles.

A smile means your checkup was great. A frown shows your smile's down in the mouth.

A smile is a self-serve lips line.

A smile is your face's express-ion line.

You can't give me a lip lock. My lips come with anti-lock brakes. They only break open with a smile.

It's nice to smile when your belly is full, but it's better to smile when you're grateful for being full of grace.

It's difficult for an artist to capture and draw out the essence of a smile. However, the artist can easily draw a smile on his or her face.

God gave us smiles to use as our walkie-talkies. When people see us smile, it's a sign that we're enjoying our walk through life.

A smile gives you a sense of security that increases along with your smile.

A smile is the Social Security number God gave us.

A smile is the Holy Spirit from God smiling from within you. Your Spirit says to release your smile and let it go forth and multiply.

A smile is an *addition* to your face that won't *negate* your chances of being *divided* on choosing the best path for your *smile* to go forth and *multiply.*

A smile says, "Please tie my shoes." When your smile's not there, it's because it's all tied up.

A frown is a smile that hasn't been tried up.

Did you ever stop to consider that your smile matches the shape of a rainbow? To complete your smile, make it just as colorful.

A smile is a moat for our mouths. The more you smile, the more you become a moat a mouth.

A smile is like a bow so your gift of a smile can be unwrapped yet still have a pretty bow.

A smile is your remote control device that says, "Let's go!" But God didn't make it remote; it's under your nose because God knows it will be easier to find when you lose it.

A smile goeth before the frown.

A smile comes first, followed by our feeling happier.

A smile is God's sign to you. It is shaped like a bow to remind you He's fulfilling His rainbow's promise to always keep you afloat during life's storms, if you have faith the size of a mustard seed that lets you muster up a smile.

A smile goeth before the banana split. It splits your smile into segments of pleasure that are seen with each bite.

A smile can goeth before the fall if you've been smiling all summer.

A sweet smile is the cane God gave you to say you are able.

A smile is a cane that supports our lame excuses.

An ounce of smiles is worth a pound of frowns.

A smile is a frown that's finally decided to be happy.

A smile is God's sign that you believe in Him, and it's your sign to others to believe in Him.

A smile says, "Happy New Year" throughout the year.

A smile makes it Christmas every day.

Knowing Christ puts a massive smile on my face, not just at Christ-mas but every day.

A smile is a pre-view-wing of God's coming attractions.

My smile was lost and now I'm frowned.

I peel my orange with a smile and notice each of its sections looks like a smile. This shows me that I, like the orange, can continue to smile even though my life feels like it's being pulled to pieces.

A smile is like freshly made juice from your main squeeze.

Die is in diet to remind you that you will if you don't.

I see a smile in every bite saying, "Don't bite off more than you can chew."

A smile helps you eat your words when you break your promise to diet.

A smile is the food that nourishes the fruit of your spirit.

A smile each day is the manna that God provides so people will say, "Manna like your style."

A smile gives each man-na bite to nourish him for a bit.

A smile gives each man-na way to give it back to God and others so we can feed off each other.

A smile gives you feedback to help you decide to send back the food they're feeding you.

A wise man first gives his smile credit for his success.

I credit a smile for reminding me that it's the only credit I want to run up and over the limited space on my face.

A smile is your credit account, on account of it making you smile when you're given the credit.

God lets you wipe the smile off your face so you will know *right* where you *left* it.

A smile on your face is the simplest change to improve the world, as well as your outlook on the world.

A smile lights up your night until the dawn breaks out another one to lighten your chores all day long.

A smile lets you know fight from calm.

A smile is a light with might that makes you strong, in your calm fight to determine right from wrong.

A smile says, "I'm right."

A smile says, "You're right."

A smile says, "Let's just say we both agree to disagree."

A smile gives you a sunny disposition, even when the sun's not shining.

A smile doesn't talk, but it says a lot about you.

Smiles are our fortune tellers- gushing forth signs of a bright, rosy future.

You don't need a crystal ball to predict a smile. Simply have a ball and smiles will crystallize all around.

Smiles have wings—no bull; I smile when I eat chicken wings with a Red Bull energy drink.

A smile is like a compass that directs you to keep your chin *up* when you're feeling *down*.

A smile is a new beginning, if you begin each new day with a smile.

Roses are red,
Violets are blue,
But without your tulips,
There's no way I could smile and kiss you.

A smile reflects your inner spirit in a light*hearted* way.

A smile says, "I'll have another."

A smile says, "I got mine from my mother."

I see my smile on Mother's Day and every day I see my mother smile.

A smile says, "I love my brother from another mother."

A smile says, "I love my sister from another mister."

A smile says you love every kind of sista and brotha.

A smile matters only if you make it a matter to smile.

I can't see my smile in the dark unless I wear my fluorescent lipstick.

A smile lets me see life through rose-colored flashes.

Your lips are red, so I can read into the smile on your lips.

My smile is my faith in the one true Light until I see a smile beaming at me when I finally see the Light.

Smiles don't come in tenses because a smile doesn't make you tense.

A smile is only tense when you make it intense.

The campers were really happy because their smiles were in tents.

Now that we have to wear face masks and can't see someone smile, we're left disappointed because we realize a smile matters in getting to know who that person really is.

A smile cracks the surface when opening a hardened heart.

A joke has been known to crack a smile.

A smile is an external sign from our inner soul that lets us know smiles are eternal.

Lips aren't needed for communicating, but a smile says I heard you.

A smile is another form of lip reading.

A smile is our face mask that lets people know how we feel or don't feel or just don't know.

A smile is your lips in sync. A smile helps you lip sync.

I smile when I listen to NSYNC.

A smile is the lipstick for your lipshtick.

When you get down, a smile helps you get up.

A smile says, "I got your back whenever you plan to come back."

A smile says, "I believe in you and I believe I can make you smile."

A smile is your face saying, "Kiss my mass."

A smile is seductive and says, "Kiss me, you fool."

A smile won't make you a fool because a fool can't make you smile; he or she is only fooling around.

It takes a comedian to make you smile or a fool who wants to make his or her living as a comedian.

A smile is your body's way of saying, "Do you like my body language?"

A smile is an easy cheer reclining on your face.

A smile says, "You had it in you all this time."

Your smile glows you better than anyone.

God put a smile on your mouth to monitor what comes out of the middle of it. That's why God spelled m-out-h with the word out in the middle.

Your smile knows you better than anyone. Make your smile glow better than anyone.

A smile can be used to put people on hold as long as you hold onto your smile.

A smile says, "I love how you hold me."

A smile is the glue that holds your face together when you crack up from being told you're stuck up.

When you lose face, don't lose your smile. It's right under your nose.

A smile is like a popsicle you break to share with someone; when you do your part and break out a smile, it's something you can share with everybody.

Clean comedian: good humor man.

I smile when I hear music from the ice cream truck.

A smile is brilliant because it makes you shine.

A smile isn't hard of hearing. A smile says, "You don't have to hear me; just see me."

A smile bears repeating. Your lips bare a smile that's worth repeating.

A smile is like a burp that's worth repeating because it makes you feel better.

A smile is our shrine that God smiles on and blesses, while I just shine you on about cutting your tresses.

Why do people smile? It's a way God gave us to acknowledge Him.

A smile is the best thing to give your mom on Mother's Day.

A smile is the best thing to pop up on Father's Day.

A smile says, "Have a nice day." A smile back says, "Thanks, I am."

A smile is like a greeting card in time of need; it's a deed that helps fill the need, and as time goes on, it's not forgotten.

A smile can help you gum up with the tooth.

A smile is an easy way to get your way.

A smile is a, "People whisperer."

A smile is your opening act, so you stanza chance of receiving an ovation.

A smile is a home run with only your gum when you have no teeth.

An infectious smile can lead to a serious case of smile-at-us.

A smile is your automatic mouth opener.

A group of *smiles* is a *party*.

I was a party to seeing my sales group smiling when they reached their goals.

Your smile comes from your very core, and hopefully leads to your being asked for an encore.

Smile when your tooth falls out. A smile can help you catch it.

A smile gets you right to the tooth.

A smile lets you get a bite on things before you eat them.

Your tooth won't fall out if you keep up your smile with a proper, proven, program of performed dental hygiene.

A smile is an entrance into your mental cavity.

Your open mouth is your oral cavity; it opened the idea of naming a rotting tooth a cavity.

A penny for your smile? No, it's priceless.

A smile is like a penny. It's cent from heaven.

It takes a village to raise a smile. It takes a smile to raise one in a village.

A smile says, "You're joking around."

A smile says, "You're not joking around."

You only have one life and one smile. Keep on expressing your smile down to your very last mile.

Smiling lips should be first on every list, especially if you have a lisp.

I place my order of food and then I order some extra C. A C is an extra smile on the side.

Vitamin C is just a smile turned on its side-splitting effect.

I smile taking my vitamins because smiles are vitamins for our spirits.

Your willingness to smile is
Pretty much up to you.
Be happy not sad.
Be glad not mad.

A smile drawn on a sure face is a line that divides happy from sad.

A smile is your brain giving you a present that's okay to reveal to others.

The best way to maintain a smile is to use it more.

A smile will grow and get bigger when you feed it with love.

A smile is the shortest line you can give.

A smile is a way for you to communicate to others that you don't feel like talking right now.

A smile is the shortest sentence, that's not sent tense, unless it's your sentence at the punitentiary.

A smile is the shortest line of communication.

A smile is a hologram of your face saying, "Hell-o Gram."

A past smile, fondly remembered, feels like I'm going back grin time.

A curt smile is just gossip grin.

Let it be a smile. Oh, let it be. A smile is the answer. Let it free, let it be.

Your smile is a mime on your face pointing out the important message that a smile is wisdom without words.

It's not important if your smile's not perfect. It's more important that your smile makes things seem more perfect.

There is no perfect smile, just a smile seeking perfection from you.

A smile is not perfect. It is always under construction.

Smiles on our faces cover the only ways to be funny.

1) We smile at funny things
2) We smile at things said in a funny way
3) We smile and look funny naked
4) We smile when a clown acts funny
5) We smile when a comedian uses funny props

You never feel naked when your revealing smile's got you covered.

A smile is the best prop your face uses to prop you up.

You don't need a green thumb to grow a big smile.

When you wipe your lips, your smile is still there until someone or something wipes it off.

A smile will bring about the notion that a mother and child reunion is only a motion away.

I feel inclined to smile after I'm declined because it makes me feel more accepted.

A smile is the fountain of hoot.

I smile again and again because a smile is a gain that pays and grows.

A smile says, "More please."

With a smile, you gain a better chance of people not being a-*gain*-st you.

God gave us smiles as remembrances of those loved ones who are absent.

A smile is a bookmark to remind us and others of the last time we met.

A smile is one thing you can give to others so they remember you. Your smile is your unlimited supply of business calling cards.

A smile is your indoor sunshine for the days there is none outdoors.

A smile says, "Some more s'mores please."

A smile is the dividing line between war and peace.

A smile is the best line to give someone.

It's best to smile when standing in line. Your smile gets longer as the line gets shorter.

I smile when I draw a line in the sand at a beautiful beach.

You're only poor when you can't afford to give a smile.

I have not but a smile to give, but I have a way to give all I got when I give a smile with love.

A smile is God's seal on your face telling others you're full of His grace.

I smile when my gas tank is full. I smile with thanks when I fulfill God's will.

A smile shows I'm holy and full of grace to write clean jokes.

A smile forms a chorus line for your teeth when you kick up your heels.

A frown is a smile that's been declined.

A smile is your face signaling others you're okay.

A smile is more appreciated after it is gone and even more so after you go.

After eating a great dinner, a smile provides a way to drink it all in.

A smile says, "I won't hold back. I won't back down because it's too late to frown back now."

A smile is the best response to rid yourself of ridicule. It says, "I'm cool."

A smile is an accepted addiction that doesn't need diction.

A smile lets your lips curl while you curl your biceps.

A smile is you curling your hair while you curl your lips.

A smile is feedback your lips provide for your face so others don't make an about face.

A smile is your radar as it's detected by others.

I am lost without my smile. That's why I don't leave home without it.

You smile when you're sick and tired of being sad.

I smile when my blood pressure is normal.

A smile helps relieve any pressure that's pushing away your happiness.

There's no whine when your smile is genuine.

I smile drinking a good wine as I drink in your smile.

A smile is your face signaling your body that it can handle the pressure.

A smile is the simplest gesture that gives the greatest pleasure.

A smile is your dental floss to prevent truth decay.

Smiles are given to signal that you are forgiven.

A smile is how your lips give a tip. Please tip generously with a smile.

A smile is one of life's little pleasures, that is being stored with our heavenly treasures.

A smile says, "Please and thank you" at the same time.

A positively great smile helps you avoid negative people.

I smile when I can see it reflected upon my newly shined shoes.

I smile when I find a comfortable shoe that fits like a glove.

A smile is never meant to hurt or step on anybody's feelings. Raising a smile helps to pick up others.

Your lips are your face's jumper cables when you need to jumpstart your smile.

A smile seals a handshake and a promise that the new medicine will stop your hands from shaking.

A smile says, "Be my Valentine."

A terrific smile tells others that you are.

I caught a glimpse of her smile, but I never caught up to her.

A smile says, "You caught my eye with your smiling eyes."

A smile says, "Hello" even before you meet.

A smile is your lips breaking out their finest face setting.

All things are possible when all things are done with a smile.

You can't borrow a smile; you have the ability to make all you need.

A smile helps you make new friends who smile, and helps you cheer up your old friends.

A smile is like glasses that can give you a better vision of your goals.

A smile says, "I can keep a secret."

I see a sea of smiling faces singing in the choir.

A smile says, "I'll hold your hand."

A smile says, "I'll give you a hand."

A smile says, "My hands are full and I need yours to help me."

A smile says, "I'll stay with you until your smile returns."

A smile accepts the blame.

A smile says, "I'm open to suggestion."

It's hard to blame someone who is always smiling.

A smile is a way for your face to make an exclamation point while you're speaking.

A smile helps to explain things.

A smile says, "Funny you should ask."

A smile says, "I don't know."

A smile is a small effort that can lead one to great accomplishments.

A smile is your promise that you will keep it.

A smile is your lighter that kindles the spark when you're rekindling relationships.

A Kindle device makes me smile as I rekindle all my favorite books at the touch of a button.

A smile reminds you to count all your blessings. It is God's will for you as He smiles down on you with His gifts from heaven.

A smile says, "I hit the mother lode."

I smile when I call and talk with my mother.

A smile reflects my mother's load of concern for my success.

A smile says, "Treat me like I want to be treated to your smile."

A smile says, "Treat not trick" at Halloween and throughout the year.

A smile is a surprise that you play on your face.

Smile when you're happy
Smile when you're sad
Be who you must It's a part of God's plan
Just know you must smile
When you see Him again

I smile when I go on vacation and my smile goes with me. I smile when I get back home because there's no place like home when you get back from your roam.

A smile says, "You are on my mind."

A smile says, "I'm getting my kicks eating my Kix cereal."

My wife's smile is up when the toilet seat is down.

It's no toil or sweat
To let your smile get
A seat on your face
That's reserved for more smiles.

Face it: I smile when I remember to keep the seat down when I leave.

A smile is a frown at ease, especially when you see brownies.

I smile because you remembered to put nuts in my brownies.

I smile when my diet is maintained by maintaining my willpower so I don't eat my brownies all at once.

A smile says, "I'm excellent, but I'm not perfect."

My smile says, "I'm perfectly excellent when you smile back at me."

Your curvy smile says, "It's slippery when wet."

A smile is a horoscope for your face that predicts a favorable future. Scope it out.

A smile is meant to be scoped out and not scooped into a frown.

I like the way your lips purse to smile when I ask for some change.

A smile says, "To be continued" so you don't have to continue to smile.

Your smile makes you a gumslinger so shoot me…a smile.

An ounce of smiles is worth a pound of frowns. Don't pound your fist and frown, just ounce back with a smile.

A smile is a fan for your mouth because it makes you a fan of others.

A smile says, "I'm doing it for me and for the sheer love of it."

I want to see if a smile will turn up when I watch my dad eat his turnip.

A smile is your body's attitude and energy gauge that shows if you're a positive person or a negative one.

A smile helps you walk the line. Hang a smile on your face and know it's one line that helps you cross the finish line.

When people get drunk in Holland, others smile and call them holland-daze or hollandaise because they're sauced.

A smile is your shingle that says, "My front door has a welcome mat."

A smile is reserved until you recover from the shingles.

I hang a smile on my face when I'm hanging ten. I hope I don't wipe off my smile when I wipe out.

A smile sponges your tears and helps hide your fears.

Aren't you glad you smiled? Don't you wish everybody did? Aren't you glad that we each control our own smile? Control yours so it makes others smile and you'll be glad you're making your wish come true.

The worst thing to own is a fr-*own*.

A smile is like fruit. It has appeal.

A smile is like citrus fruit. A smile says, "Orange you glad to see me?"

A smile helps you deal with the lemons life hands you so you can smile while you make lemonade.

A smile says, "Life will get better. I just have to suck it up and keep smiling."

Flexing your lips to form a smile is the easiest exercise you can do.

It takes seventeen muscles to smile and forty-three muscles to frown. It's so much easier to smile and be happy than to frown and be sad. The best break you can give your face is to break into a strong, confident smile.

A smile helps to keep you in touch with both sides of your face. Just don't let people know you're two faced.

Sometimes a smile says, "I can't decide which side of my face is my best side." I think any side with a smile is your best side.

When you see a smile being reflected, it allows your smile to feel like it's beside itself.

Your smile reflected off a surface is good because it means you're smiling. Your smile reflected on another's face is best because it means you've made a potential friend.

A smile says, "I've only heard your side, and I know there's two sides to how things happen."

A smile gives you time to arrange your thoughts so you can give an answer that throws them a curve using only that sneaky, curved smile of yours.

A smile is a treasure chest full of gold coins you can spend to get what you desire; it will be replenished at your will for the rest of your life.

A smile gets us the priceless treasures in life: 1) the love of God and Jesus 2) our health and spirit and 3) our families. It doesn't cost a cent to obtain them.

My favorite four-letter word is *free*. You are always free to smile because it doesn't cost; it pays to smile freely

A smile just says, "I'll be happy to accompany you to the dessert aisle on your desert isle."

The scent of a woman attracted me to her lips smiling the message, "Penny for your thoughts." I thought her smile looked de-cent.

A smile completes the painting of a colorful masterpiece that was painted by humans but created by God.

Your smile is your moon shadow. When the lights are low and no moon is out, your smile is.

When a child asks why, a smile says, "Because I said so."

A smile is a time-out for your brain.

A smile lets you mull over and sift out words from your mouth.

I was at a loss for words and then I smiled. That seemed to say it all.

A smile is a microcosmic catalyst to stimulate God's plan and purpose for your life.

A smile says, "My lips were sucking on an ice-cold Slurpee."

I lost my smile, but when I went to the lost and frowned, it was nowhere to be found.

A smile on your lips tells others you won't give them any lip.

A smile on your face is your best tactic to ensure the relationship is moving forward.

A smile is the only lip service you should render.

When you play tennis, smile before you serve an ace. Even if you lose, a smile can always serve as your ace.

Smile and the whole world smiles with you. Frown and no one will be frowned with you.

Keep a smile on your way to work. Keep a smile at work, and don't be a jerk.

Smile before you go to bed and rest your weary little head.

A ready smile is the best pre-fix to add as an aid to getting you out of a fix.

My smile is my wingman for meeting new friends.

My smile reflects the image of God's smile.

A smile is the best way to save face, so you learn you'll get 'em next time.

Serving with a smile is the best way to serve or give service to anyone or anything.

A smile is a takeout delivery order from your face, delivered by your lips that smile when you open the box.

New app for comedy: smileyfacebook

A smile spreads our lips to stress a point without causing stress to those people our smile is pointed at.

A smile says, "The worst is over and my best life ever is just ahead."

You are the only one who can stand behind your smile. It stands for who you are.

Gesture a smile; nothing else is needed to convey happiness.

A smile is a gesture way to be happy being a jester.

I smile when the weekend arrives.

I smile when it's Sunday, my favorite day of the week.

You must muster a smile each and every day.

We need to designate an official National Smile Day.

Smile with purpose and pride even if you smile by accident.

A frown is a deflated smile, not a defeated smile.

A smile is a feat you can perform regardless of your feet, except if your foot is in your mouth.

Did I catch you with a smile? A smile can carry you through. I guess a smile is your lips' way to catch and carry what it wants.

A smile is your face's address that's freely given to those people you address.

A smile is your seasoning to make you more tasteful during any season.

A smile makes it easier to practice what you breach.

God gave you a smile to lift you up like wings as you watch your life fly by.

A smile lets you talkie while you walkie off the pounds as you earn bonus time for a treat.

Your smile is a summation of your viewpoint while you're multi-tasking. A repeated smile is multi-asking.

A dazzling smile is your one shining moment that outshines what you say.

When I fast, I can write my jokes faster.

A smile helps you eat the words of others and aids you even more so when you have to eat your own.

A smile is like the fruit of the whine.

Whine is not the spirit of a smile.
A spirited smile says you don't drink wine.

A smile is like an uplifting wind that helps you win as you wind on down the road.

A smile is your telescope that you can adjust to clear the vision of your goal to the point where you see yourself smiling.

Smile that smile
The one that goes for miles and miles
The smile that's got me thinking of you
That's what you gotta do.

Have a hunger to smile and use tasteful words so it will be a tasty treat if later you find you have to eat them.

A smile is a picture entitled 'Silence is Golden.'

A frown is a smile's Twisted Sister caught looking downward.

If you're the butt of a joke, just smile and realize that a butt crack is a smile and it's your bottom line.

Q: How do we know our smiles were meant for *us*?

A: Just look at your smile and see:
1) It's glamor-o-*us*;
2) It's gorge-o-*us*; and best of all
3) It gets *us* together.

My smile is my oldest and bestest friend in the whole wide world.

Don't tell me to forget about it. I want you to smile.

A smile indicates your demeanor: the more it decreases, da-meaner you get.

A smile requires no deposit because you have instant checking. Go ahead and check; you'll see you can smile in an instant because you're full of smiles, even though you don't know who keeps depositing them. You'll always feel fulfilled with a smile.

A smile is an original that has seen no improvements or advancements since the dawn of humankind; it never will, because God made it perfect.

A smile is only genuine when it's your will to do God's and it's being confirmed by your smile.

A smile needs no compliments. Your smile already compliments you in the best of ways.

A smile helps make humankind more kind.

A genuine smile says your intentions are genuine.

A smile is your tent. God provides for your con-tent-men-t. It's no con; a tent was what God meant to cover your face in the form of a smile. Your smile is a sign that Jesus's death covered and sealed your salvation. Your smile indicates that you know you have God's Spirit.

A smile is the entrance to your earthly home. God says that your earthly home houses the Holy Spirit, the Holy of Holies, who is heavenly sent to remodel your tent until it turns into His temple.

A smile says, "Ding-dong, I'm here."

A smile says, "I have an accent because I'm from Boston."

It's no accident.
God gave you a smile
To accent your face and
Accentuate your personality, so
It's more like His son's.

A smile is no accident;
It's the best dent that's
Indented on your face.

A smile is understood by people of all languages, even if they speak with an accent. All people understand that a smile speaks louder and clearer than words.

A smile is your solemn promise to keep your mouth shut.

A smile is your accent. It accentuates your personality. It speaks without needing words or an accent to accentuate the fact that your smile is all that's needed.

A smile is a dent on your face that you use as a tool to help smooth out all the dents you'll face in life.

An ounce of smile will produce a pound of cure-osity.

A smile is a dent on my face that says, "I'm God's indent-ured servant."

A smile serves us in time of need, especially when we serve others in need.

A smile is one of God's wills for your life, and it is meant to last a lifetime.

Where there's a smile, there is a way that will show up when you glow up.

A smile says, "Yeah, I'll show up."

Seeing you ponder which smile you'll wear today gives me a good picture of how your day will develop.

Smile when you wake up to this day that the Lord has made for you to enjoy.

A smile is a sign of God's grace etched on our faces. It's our humble sign to others that we are thankful for Him and His blessings.

Start your day with a smile. You'll see that your day is already starting to look up.

A smile says, "Everything is turning up roses" as you smile at the Rose Parade.

I smile when I visit other countries, and I notice that my smile can go on for a country mile in any country.

The habit of always having a smile is not hard to pick up. Just start by picking up your lips.

The habit of smiling is not hard to acquire when you find that it makes it easier to acquire exactly what you want.

I managed to amass a smile as the masseuse massaged my pain and it miraculously went away.

A smile says, "You're not serious." I say, "It's serious if you don't smile."

A smile says, "Don't worry; it's not serious."

I hope you turn up with your smile as you're headed to heaven. You'll surely frown when you learn you're going down.

When you smile, you are encouraged to tell your problems that they're going down like a frown. Your smile finally taught you it's your best way of not letting them get you down.

I smile when I go up the escalator. It seems to make the ride more uplifting. I smile when I go down the escalator. I only frown when using the stairs.

A smile helps with the pain when you trip on the stairs and fall. Remember not to stare and trip all over yourself with a painful look when she smiles, stares into your eyes, and says, "I'm falling for you."

A smile says, "I have a big surprise and you're looking at it."

A smile says, "I'm surprised when I don't see you smiling."

A smile breaks out on my face when the puck goes in the net on the faceoff.

A smile says, "I'm glad to see your smile is gleed to see mine."

A smile is a crease sliding in the grease on your face hoping to save you from being a disgrace.

God gave us grace,
And He gave us smiles
To grace our faces.
And when they are not there,
You show God you dis Him.
God says it's a disgrace to not
smile and throw His grace into His face.

Lend a smile during the Lenten season knowing Jesus is the reason.

A smile is that space on your face that isn't out of place, even if you orbit outer space.

A smile is a promise that reaches the moon and the stars when it is dark. Its promise is fulfilled with each rising sun, which enlightens our minds that a smile is the light that lightens our burdens.

A smile says, "My burden is easy as I smile at your yokes."

Your smile is your signal to God that His burden is easy and His yoke is light.

My yoke is easy and my burden is light when ere my smile is beaming bright.

I smile and yolk around while eating my eggs sunny side up.

When I come over, it's easy to smile and order my eggs over easy.

If you throw eggs with a smile, they'll know you're just yolking.

I smile when I sit on my porch. I smile when I sit in a Porsche.

I smile when I drive around in my Porsche because I feel like no one is gonna Porsche me around.

A smile says, "Take your time. I'll wait until you are done."

A smile says, "I believe I was here first." It's as obvious as the smile on my face.

My smile says, "I'm happy I came in first because I first started my preparations with a smile."

You inherited your smile from God as a forecast of your future with Him.

I smile when my lawyer calls and says my uncle left me an inheritance.

Your smile is a good inheritance to leave your children.

Teaching your children to smile is the best chance that they'll remember you when they smile.

Pass on a smile before you pass on giving one. Please do it before you pass on.

A smile says, "I filled one of your needs by pulling your weeds."

A smile says, "You smoked weed."

I think therefore I spam.

If it ain't broke, then don't break it. If you do break it, then you better break out a smile.

You'll never appreciate your smile until it's taken away from you by some frown.

I guess that frown got you to appreciate your smile.

We have pedometers to tally our steps. We need grin-meters to number our daily smiles.

I smile when my face mask is forgotten;
I smile more when they don't ask.
It's a simple task to go get a new one.
I smile and don't feel rotten,
Knowing my mistake is forgotten.

If a smile is the only thing you can give that person, give it well and freely knowing you left the world better off.

Smiling is a habit that's easy to develop when it's pictured on others.

A smile says, "I won't stop trying until I succeed."

Some sinners are saved after countless sermons from countless pastors. However, a simple, sincere smile has helped save many more sinners.

A weak smile was found in his sour disposition because his smile was in a bad position.

Your smile is the best you-turn for getting back on the road to success.

It isn't a sin to smile. It is a sin if you don't smile more.

A smile got you a good appointment.
You got a smile for being prompt.
You provided a smile before you gave your pitch.
You got a smile back to say they're open.
Keep on smiling and the deal will be closed.

A smile is more important than any problem.

A smile says, "I have no doubt."

Smile when you count your blessings. Remember to include your smile.

When I smile, I still feel good even if my smile isn't returned.

A smile every day leads to multiple smiles every week, month, and year until you realize the millions of smiles you've experienced are what constitute abundant living.

A smile says, "We can always try a grin tomorrow."

A smile may be the only blessing and opportunity you get today. It is totally worth embracing.

A smile is the softest tool to fix a hardened heart.

A *good* one-word message is "smile."
A *better* one-word message is "listen."
The *best* one-word message is "love."
Now act on these messages and smile and listen with love.

A smile helps to get over a disaster much faster.

The older I get, the more I appreciate each new day, my friends, my health, and my ability to smile.

When I want to impress, I'm gonna press a smile on my face.

When under pressure, a smile gets you over being tired so you persist until it's relieved and everyone smiles.

I smile during my darkest moments, and I smile even more when my power is restored.

It is far better to smile than to not do so. Without a smile you won't get far.

A smile is best even if you have nothing to say. It's also best when you do.

Our smiles let others take their eyes off their problems and see that we have overcome our problems successfully many times in our lives.

It's no work to smile, and a smile can get you work that you want.

A smile can help you pass the test.
A smile needs no learning or study.
A smile just needs to be applied to any test you face in your work, family, and relationships to bring about your desired result.

A smile is a goal that's plainly in sight.
It takes minimal effort so God could make sure you'd get it right.

You don't have to be great
To have a great smile.
Just have a smile that helps
Others to smile and
You're on your way to being great—
Especially if you want to be
A great comedian.

I smile when I get a good opportunity, and I make it a point to smile at every opportunity.

A smile says, "I care."

A smile is mirth overcoming your worries and cares.

A smile appears when a solution is found. It was found that smiling makes solutions occur quicker.

If you don't smile much and you try to smile more each day, you'll find people will have more confidence in seeing that you're on the level when your smile is turned up.

When you arrive with love and a smile, you gain instant acceptance.

I've never heard of a single smile that was drowned out by another smile. A smile helps keep you afloat.

A smile can't die from dehydration because it's no sweat to smile.

It's your fate to smile when you're late and when you're foolish.

One advantage to giving or watching a smile is your hands can be busy doing other things, like holding someone and kissing him or her.

It should be your ambition to smile. A smile is the mother of invention. A smile leads to a solution, all because you smothered them with your smile.

Don't just *sit* there and do nothing. A smile is something you could do to put you in good *stand*ing.

Don't just wish you could smile. By just attempting it you might see that your wish came true.

A smile says, "Be of good cheer." Be thankful you didn't fall off the chair.

I smile smelling grandma's strawberry preserves and the lingering aroma preserves my smile.

And eye for an eye leaves one blind. A smile for a smile leaves one with a friend.

A smile is success that's easily achieved.

I smile when I'm lucky. Luck may change, but giving a smile won't change whether I'm lucky or not. You're lucky to just be able to smile.

A smile is worth taking a risk that it won't make anyone upset.

A smile is the best gift to return.

A smile says, "I stand for you and behind you if you fall or fail."

If you can't smile at yourself, there's still hope that you can go out and do something else that makes you smile.

A smile is a pause that refreshes when you got no money for refreshments.

In the long run, you may not have any achievements greater than others. But you can achieve a smile that is greater than all others.

A smile is a small line out on your face that outlines where you're headed.

It doesn't cost you to give people a sincere smile. It pays to know you can't afford not to smile.

A smile shows you are in love when everyone says they love your smile.

We don't have to guess if we're smiling. A smile is easy to spot. You're left with no pout about it.

I'm opening a smile factory that's called Smile Productions. We have openings.

A smile is your unmistakable trademark. Don't trade that mark for all the money in the world.

I smile playing golf and I smile knowing why I play golf. Golf gives me a legitimate excuse to approach women with a smile and ask, "Do you want to play a round?"

Being willing to smile, though you're incapable, is acceptable. Being physically able to smile, yet not willing, is reprehensible.

A smile says, "I did my best; now the rest is up to God."

Instead of pointing a finger, hold out your hand to help while giving them a smile.

A smile is totally under your guidance and responsibility.

There is no wrong way to smile, so smile — it's your right.

It's easy to perform and give a smile. Performing a smile is what a person does so he or she looks his or her best.

I believe little of what I hear and a lot of what I see. When I see your smile, however, I truly and fully believe in you.

Our family was so poor that we exchanged loving smiles as gifts at Christmas.

A smile is the best thing to give before you're given another chance.

Smile at everyone, even if they don't smile back. Your smile is encouragement for them to correct their mistake of not smiling.

Smile even if people don't remember what you said. A smile can be unforgettable.

A smile is for giving when I'm forgiven.

Never judge someone's smile, but remember: someone is judging yours.

A smile is the easiest to
Accomplish and acquire,
And is most profitable for
Fulfilling your desires.

A smile on your face gives you courage to face…anything.

A smile is like a library book. It gets checked out and you hope it's not long overdue.

A smile lets you put your face on smile holding or waiting or forwarding to confirm you'll answer the call.

Was that a smile from your lips blowing me a kiss, or did you just sneeze?

A smile is an expression you can reserve for your face so it never loses its seat on your lips.

A smile emoji is nothing compared to the qualities of a human smile.

A smile is like word of mouth with just the mouth and no lip.

A "swoosh" is Nike's smile of success.

You can dress someone up fancy, but you don't need to clothe that smile on your face. You ain't dressed if you ain't got a smile.

Smiles are bow ties for our faces. A smile is a beau tied in laces.

A smile is your face giving your cheek a karate chop.

It's so nice to blow a smile. Don't blow it by not smiling.

A smile says, "You're on the right path even if you get stepped on."

Don't trash your smile. Have it on when you take out the trash.

In this digital age, no digits are needed to smile.

I smile when I get to order takeout. A smile is your face's takeout order—order one or more now and for always.

A smile is a meet and greet drive thru for you to drive home a point.

A smile is calling and waiting for one to be returned.

A smile is not digital or analog. It is a special formatting of the face. I *dig-it*. Smile, *an-a-log* will light your fire.

Your smile is like an LED light:
Life Eternally Displayed.

Your smile always works — with no downtime.
No glitches just glimpses,
No clicks just licks —
A smile is a screamsaver for your face.
No plug needed. Just paste one on your mug and see the power glow.
A smile doesn't crash if you sleep with a smile on your face.

A smile is your tongue's *lap*top.

Smile and face it, as it's the first thing people see on your face.

I smile when I read my Kindle. A smile is the best way to kindle a kiss.

I see a smile as a *C* lying on its back as I lie on my back at the beach, looking at the sea.

A smile is an easy way to get in touch without having to touch.

A smile doesn't have an accent. It just accent-uates your look.

We don't smile at accidents, but sometimes we smile accidentally.

It's no accident that smiles don't have accents. I mean, it goes without saying.

You had me at your smile.

I beat him by a smile.

A smile is the best way to keep your lips closed until the deal is closed.

We have the answers for the problems of others, but none for our own. If we but own a smile on our faces, we begin to see those others smiling back at us, and the answer soon appears from our peers.

A smile is a tune up for your lips to say, "Turn up that tune."

Smile, knowing you're led by the Spirit of God.

A smile is the way your face surprises itself.

At a resort, your enjoyment is heightened when you resort to smiling.

Be patient and smile while you're waiting in line. It puts you in good standing.

A smile needs no content or context. It already says you are content.

A smile will always be with us.

You're only poor if you can't afford to smile.

Kind thoughts give wisdom,
Kind words give hope,
Kind deeds create love —
Kinda like a smile does all that.

It's not what you know about your smile, it's what you do with your smile.

A smile is your body's high beam indicator giving you a clearer path to your future.

Don't stop smiling when you're old. You got old because you stopped smiling.

I was joshed and now I'm frowned.

You will be lost if a smile is frowned.

Smiles are our happy meters. I'm happy to mete one out and say, "Glad to meet ya."

I was surfing on Google and found a new comedy website. It's called Giggle.

A smile is all you need to get by.
A smile is all you need for a good-bye.
A smile is all you need to get the Best Buy.

A smile says, "I'll try."

A smile is a curve that can straighten things out.

Irish eyes are smiling when ere glasses of rye are piling.

Babies smile in utero because they get womb service.

Her smiling stringing you along is the only string she's got left to play.

A smile is a feat to mete, when we meet and you step on my feet.

A smile needs no words, not because it's unheard of; it's just more seenly that way.

A smile is a permanent facial feature. You're stuck up without it being stuck to your face, so just grin and bare it.

Our thankful smiles after saying grace mean more to God than all the food we stuff in our faces.

There is innate power in a smile. It makes your face feel more energized.

A smile says, "I'm not gonna cry."

A smile makes us appear more highbrow as others appear and say, "Hi bro!"

A smile dares not go where drools rush in.

A smile on your face will not rest if your chin is on your chest.

A smile means the same in any language, race, or creed.

A smile is all that matters
As it splatters
When your joke bombs.

A smile says, "I'm talking here. Read my lips."

It's better to let them see your smile and let them wonder than to open your mouth and see them smile, because now they know.

A smile is very supportive because it helps you stand out.

When my smile is wry, I get a shot of rye whiskey.

Your smile can go on tour; just be sure to smile wherever you go.

I possess a smile I do not own. It is a treasure owned by God and temporarily on loan as an exhibit hosted by my face.

I feel God's love more when I smile and remember that with God, all things are possible.

I smile knowing God's presence is the greatest of all His presents.

I smile when my dog licks my face. My dog knows it's my way of licking his face.

I smile while riding the crest of a wave that's curling as big as my smile.

God made light much faster than sound, so people can see your smile before you utter a sound.

Retirement makes me smile when the only thing I cross out on my daily to-do list is the day.

A smile is the best line to run up your face during a race, signaling you crossed the finish line first.

A smile is a sponge to soak up the tears that run down your cheeks when ere your eyes begin to leak.

A smile and a frown
Form the dichotomy found
When they form a circle to remind us
Of our journey on the circle of life.

A smile helps you stay happy when your opponent has a snappy final reply.
Your peace is maintained because your smile's not awry.

A smile changes frowns over pounds into smiles over fewer ounces that tip the scales in your favor.

A smile takes a second, but is remembered for hours.

A smile is a loaner vehicle to use until you acquire your own. It's the lease you can do.

A smile needs no content. You can just smile if you're content.

A smile is a friend who best fits your *person*-ality.

Do everything with a smile. Go ahead, you got time.
You weren't doing anything anyway!

I'm infatuated with that big fat smile you just waited to give me.

A smile washed over my face which was submerged in water, being cleansed by God's Spirit as I was baptized.

A smile is a mistake eraser that also helps ease a racer.

A smile goes without saying.

A smile is saying, "Yeah, there he goes!"

God seated your smile perfectly so it could always be relaxed and up front.

Candy is dandy,
But snicker is quicker.
Hey, Snickers are dandy candy.

I saw a smile in my *rear*view mirror,
So I pulled to the *side*
And had her sit up *front*.

This jest in the news:
Smiling and laughing are
Good for your health;
It's mirth trying.

I smile while doing Tai chi
As I drink my Chai tea.

A smile is your face's hi beam headlight.

A smile is an appetizer,
And it's a foretaste of the main dish.

Smilitis is miles and miles of smiles.

Hanging around other smiles could lead to smile at us.

A smile is your song. It's one way of praising Him with your hymn.

A smile is the front door of your temple. Keep it open.

If your smile is your temple's entrance, make it entrancing.

A smile is a way for your spirit to keep the light on in your temple.

Bone up on your smiling,
Just don't get
Osteo-smilitis.

Our body is an unlimited smile factory that's only limited by our attitudes.

A frown is a defective smile that is usually rejected.

Don't just smile because it's happy hour. Smile every hour and be happy!

A smile is Silly Putty for your face because it comes in all shapes and sizes.

A smile on hand is your five-digit ZIP code.

Don't cover up your smile because your smile's got you covered.

If God appeared and I saw Him, I would be left speechless. God gave me a smile so I could express my essence when I see Him.

Faith is like a strong desire or wish without seeing any action. God meant faith to be a smile with action.
Your smile can be that one, small action expressing your faith.

Have faith that you could move others to smile, even though mountains of effort by others have failed. Smile when you tell them they should move to the mountains.

When you smile, you look so pretty.
When you don't smile, you're pretty ugly.

The science of smiling should be called smilonology.

I smile when I see two more.
I *don't* smile when I see tumor.
I frowned two more tumors.

Adam asked Eve what they were having for dinner. Eve smiled and replied, "Spare ribs."

I smile while camping. I don't smile while cramping.

A smile is something that approaches perfection, especially when mine approaches yours and yours approaches mine.

The smile on God's face is found on the faces of all His creations.

Talking to Siri or Alexa just isn't the same as talking to someone who is smiling.

A smile is a bow tie on your face that you don't even have to clip on. Just turn your smile on automatically.

The *Mona Lisa* was painted with no eyebrows and a minimal smile. I guess da Vinci decided to give her the brush off.

Notebook 2

You're more noted and noticed if you smile.

Ultimately, I sat down and edited my rambling thoughts about a smile. They made me smile and laugh and ponder how small things play such large roles in our lives. I don't really know for sure where all these smiley thoughts came from. Where do our thoughts come from? I know that for me, all my good ones come from above, from our very Creator.

People started to notice me as I smiled at what I had compiled thus far. If you pay me, I'll come up with as many smile jokes, puns, and anecdotes as you care to stomach. As I shared some of my one-liners with people, they were encouraged to read larger samples of my work. I smiled because people gave me good feedback concerning my book. Basically, it uplifted their spirits. They said my words made them smile. They went from being sad to being glad. Does a smile help in the healing of our bodies? I think so. I know it helps to renew our spirits. I want my words to heal the body like vitamins. I know words are powerful and help heal the spirit. My words made people smile and feel better on their unique journeys through this earthly plane. The power of one word may hold the difference between life and death.

God's plan
In this *plane*
Was to form the *planet*
And the *planets.*
Was this an accident or
Did God just planet that way?

Ultimately, our living will be judged by our giving of goodness, not greatness.

You're not poor when you're out of money, just when you're out of hope. Gee, I hope I get that loan.

You had better be on the level if you aim to hit the goals you have targeted.

The biggest liar is the devil. The next biggest liar is our memories.

It's not what you know, it's what you do with what you know; and you know you should be smiling.

An excuse is just another mistake.

It took me a long time to get it all together. Now I'm too old to lift it.

You're more likely to succeed if you stay on your toes and keep off other people's.

The most beautiful thing you can wear is a smile.

A discussion: exchange of knowledge; an argument: exchange of ignorance.

The most common human ailment is cold feet.

The road to success is not a highway; it's more like a try way.

I'm not always able to find help, but I'm able to give it.

My mind's greatest power is the ability to forget.

Some people spread happiness wherever they go. Some people spread happiness when they go.

Worries occur when we think about things. Solutions occur when we think things out.

What's a smile? It's God's kiss on our lips.

A smile is our body's "mood meter."

Life is like a smile. It is what you make it during the ups and downs of life.

If you have a smile, you'll be able to walk that extra mile.

Do you know how to take a smile and turn it into a mile? Take off the s.

It's nice to smile from ear to ear. It's not nice to smile at my big ears.

A bride's smile can light up a groom.

If a frown is a smile turned upside down, I guess frowning is the only downside to smiling.

A smile is one of the simplest forms of communication. No words are needed. Gesture smile is required.

When you see a smile, it means you're not in any trouble.

God gave us smiles so we would have keys to unlock our hearts.

The best makeup is applying a smile to your face.

A smile is a gift from God that I really enjoy returning.

What does a smile cost? I don't know — I think it's priceless.

Everyone's smile is equal because we can all smile from ear to ear.

Smiling is the best way to stop a fight because you can't beat having a great smile.

A grin is a smile away from success.

A smile is a bridge joining two or more hearts.

Your smile is a laser that can easily melt my heart.

I frown when a fly is on my face and I smile when I face the fact that my fly is down.

A smile is the beginning of the solution to a problem, and it was always right under your nose.

A smile is the easiest thing to make.

A smile can sway others to do it your way.

A wisecrack can lead you to crack a smile.

The best way to raise a smile is to ask for a raise.

A smile helps us see lip through the cracks.

A smile is our tell-a-vision.

A smile says, "You can grin and bare lip."

A smile helps us to give better lip service.

You can be poor but still have a million dollar smile.

Even if you have nothing to give, you can always give a smile.

A smile is God's way of reminding you to be upright with your lips.

A smile is the best lipstick; it is not likely to wipe off.

A smile is the highest eye cue you can attain.

A smile can reveal your eye cue.

If you lose your smile, you won't find it in the lost and frowned.

A smile is God's way of gracing our lips.

A smile is jest the birth of mirth.

A smile is the best lip calm you can apply.

We have countless reasons for failure, but we don't have a single excuse for failing to smile.

A smile can separate truce from friction.

Smiling is the best way to part your lips so you can play your part when your loved ones are de-parting.

The best part of your lips is that you can part them and smile.

A smile is better than any last word.

A smile is your last glance to look good.

It takes forty-three muscles to frown and only seventeen muscles to laugh. That's why frowning is the only exercise some people get.

I left my frown smiles away from me.

A frown is just a smile away.

A smile is doing it mime way.

Smiles are in fetch us.

A smile is just a wise crack.

A smile is laughter envisioned.

If a joke makes you smile, a smile is a good way to make a joke out of all your problems.

A smile can't go out of fashion because it always suits your style.

A frown is just a face shun statement.

A slip of the tongue produces laughter. A split of the lip produces a smile.

Our lips form smiles to remind us that the best solution is turning up.

A smile melts the miles between me and God.

Smilence is a smile without laughter.

God gave us smiles so we couldn't tell Him we had nothing to give.

To me, all smiles are a like.

I can smile in any language.

A smile is our face's sign language.

Two lips produce a smile whenever they get tulips.

A smile is the best lip service, for getting the best service.

A smile is jest up to you.

A smile is a visible reflection of our inner, unseen souls.

A smile reminds us we're eternal beings. We'll go on for smiles and smiles.

Smiles are the fruits of our souls.

A smile needs no words; instead, it provides you with an attractive picture that draws you in.

A smile is the pitch-cure perfect solution for yelling.

A smile can cure anger and yelling.

My smile has deja vu because it knows where it's beam.

Smiling makes me happy. Not smiling makes me hapless.

A smile assures me that I'm be grinning to see delight.

A smile is the brightest beam to help delight our way.

A smile holds your tongue back.

If you can't smile at yourself, it's a sad reflection on you.

Life's journey is easier if it's taken a smile at a time.

Laughter has no side effects, just side splitting effects.

I told my doctor I was allergic to laughter. On my allergy list he wrote, "No joke."

Girls only smile at me because it's quicker to snicker.

I smile more as the jeers go by.

I know what it tease that makes you smile.

A smile puts me at tease.

A smile is what it tease.

You don't need a joke to smile; in fact, it's a joke if you don't smile.

I don't do morning breakfast comedy shows because they have a two egg and a two Eggo minimum. I asked why. They said, "Because the yolks on you."

A smile will never give you the shaft even if it's mine.

God smiles when you smile.

Pout-ralysis is a failure to smile.

It helps to smile when you're really old and when you're on your way pout.

A smile takes away all doubt about pout.

Old jokes: Yore kidding.

I'm qualified to be a comedian because my whole life has been a joke.

A smile can warm an icy glare.

Past smiles: Yore grinning. Current smiles: Same Old Smiles.
Future smiles: Onward to grin-finity and beyond.

In negotiating, the one with the biggest smile wins.

A smile can be passed around the world.

A smile is our thank you to God.

A smile adds to your aware-nice and it's nice to aah wear.

Smiles have caused accidents.
But we don't smile by accident.

A grin is only a half-smile long.

Just a grin and tonic please. I don't drink, but I'm drinking in your smile.

Most people fail because they're on the path of least persistence.

I want to change the world, but so far it's only changed me.

A smile helps you keep a stiff upper lip.

A smile is uplipping to others.

A smile is the line to the divine.

A smile is a mask for aches and pains.

Smile and thou shalt receive.

Smiles are seeds that grow your grin.

A smile is the spark that lights our imaginations.

You don't have to learn how to smile, just when to smile.

When in doubt, smile.

It's best to start the day with a smile even before you get out of bed.

A smile is a new be grinning

People always smile when they're drinking; for some it's a *bar* grin.

The value of a smile is determined by how you purse your lips.

A smile is a bar grin courtesy of the gal sitting across from you.

A smile may leave you with an oh pun opinion.

Not everyone can be a great thinker, talker, writer, or doer, but everyone can smile.

Smiles are your calling cards when you are dealing with people.

Lips are useful for calling attention to our beautiful smiles.

Look before you leap and smile before you speak.

A smile is a shot of en*courage*ment.

When you smile at your enemies, you're more likely to restore the balance of power.

Smile and you've lost nothing.
Don't smile and nothing will last.

Kids laugh 200 times per day.
Adults laugh five times a day.
No wonder we call them kids and grown ups are called adults.
Grown-ups are just ah-dull-tttt-s.

Each smile is unique, so to speak.

A smile is to be seen and not hurt.

A smile is our glow button.

A smile helps hu-mor than anything.

A smile is a new beginning, or a smile is jest you grinning.

A human tongue is used for lip floss.
A human smile provides the lip gloss.

Smiles are produced by each other's actions, and they are actions to produce in others.

A smile shows you care face to face.

A smile is music on the lips.

A smile is music for the tiffs.

A smile is like medicine when you're sick.

A smile lets others know there's hope.

A smile is a repossessed and repositioned frown.

A smile is a recircled frown.

If you smile in the dark, it will be de-light.

Q: What do you call it when someone smiles while alone in the forest?
A: I call it *tree mend ous.*

The quarter moon is God smiling at night.
God is smiling because He's mooning you.

A smile is a sure sign of cheer fullness.

A smile is important for every fun.

We are all dealt the same smile.
We should play with it more often.

A smile is a crack that can put us on track.

You're more likely to be matchless when you light up your smile.

When you're outmatched, always light up with a smile.

Smiles matter and shouldn't make people madder.

Smiling can be an addiction that needs no diction added.

A smile lets us know there's still hope that you'll keep smiling.

A smile is the only crack that shouldn't be faulted.

A smile provides interest that you can bank on.

Jest not lest you be jest told more jokes.

A smile says, "I'm jest blessed."

A smile is the icing on your caked-on makeup.

A smile is nicing on the scape.

A smile is only whim deep.

A smile lets others know which side of you is up, and not what you're up to.

A smile on the *front* of your face gets people to be on your *side*.

With a smile out *front,* others are more likely to smile *back.*

A smile is like fuel for the fool when you're having a gas.

A smile is the dessert that's served in the punch-line.

My dentist only tells me to open and smile when I pull out my wallet to pay his bill.

A smile depends on our frame of mind. My smile should be in the Hall of Frame.

A smile is a sight for sore guys.

A smile can align your frame of mind.

You're only a smile away from achieving your goals.

A smile is about as close as I want to get to some people.

In the pandemic, our smiles were masked, but we still kept smiling although we were not asked.

A smile is finding good in a fault.

A smile is meant to crack you up.

A smile is a front for going behind your back.

Smile freely. It comes at no cussed to you.

A smile helps us spring out of bed after sleeping on a lumpy mattress.

I've frowned that it pays to smile.

A smile can show your style as you walk that extra mile.

When you're old, your smile shouldn't diminish.

Botox gives your smile a new wrinkle because now it's the only wrinkle.

People who give a smile a minute don't have to rush a mile a minute.

A smile is the easiest thing we can exercise.

A smile heralds an open mind and a closed mouth.

Exercise your lips by smiling more. It's guaranteed to make your smile bigger.

A smile turns your tongue from being a lap stick into being slapstick.

If you step out with a smile, you're less likely to have a slip of the tongue.

A smile is more important in failure than in success.

A smile should provide the first success after every failure.

Smiles are the fallout when we're having a blast.

A smile is a re-adjusted frown.

God gave us smiles to put our tongues on hold.

A smile is a porch light for the body.

A smile is the best face-lift.

Smiles are our happy meters.

We have not yet found a new or better way to smile, but we can smile and be thankful that all things are new every morning.

A smile is a gift you hope everyone returns.

You don't have to practice smiling; just make it your practice to smile.

A smile increases your face value when it draws interest.

If smiling was an Olympic event, we could have quarter smilers, half smilers, and people who just do the smile.

A smile is a grin to help you win.

A smile is a lost frown that finally turns up.

Clocks reveal that the secret of life is keeping your hands busy — or at least your fingers if your clock is *digit*al.

A smile expresses desire without an attempt at doing anything.

Smiling back is the best revenge.

It's easier to smile and keep people guessing what you're up to.

Gloom service is not smiling.

Smiles were sculpted to fit our skulls.

You can smile without reading the instructions on how to do it.

If smiles were used as money, you would have a poor excuse for being frowned that you're broke.

Give a smile. It's the most priceless gift you can give.

A smile is God's masterpiece that helps you to master having peace.

A smile is the cure for being down in the mouth.

Smiles are our Facebook marks.

They can smile in your face but they can't take your place because your smile is all your own.

A new smile is great, but your smile is meant to be used.

A smile is the shortest distance between two people.

A smile is the best line you could give someone.

A smile is a scene not heard.

There are no laws against smiling.

A smile is America's Most Wanted.

A smile is a grin to help you bare it and bear it.

A smile is your way of saying you're pout of words.

A smile will never go pout of style.

Remember, it's okay to text while you're smiling.

You can't forget where your smile is. You can only forget to smile.

A smile is our body's way of texting, "I love you."

A smile says, "I've got time for a while."

A smile is your face's way of checking up on your brain.

They could not convict her for smiling, but her smile was arresting.

Your face takes a turn for the better when your frown turns into a smile.

A smile is your face doing magic tics.

A smile is the way your face cheeks up on itself.

Nothing speaks louder than a smile.

A smile is your face saying, "I'm up ahead."

A smile is the best answer when people ask you what you're up to.

If not for smiles, our faces would not be what they are cracked up to be.

A smile is the best head line ever.

It sure makes head lines when we see our faces getting wrinkles.

A smile puts a new wrinkle on things.

A smile is the best wrinkle to have.

A smile makes you divine for de moment.

A smile means you want to be held. A frown means you're being held up.

A smile is the best way for your face to make a U-turn.

It's okay if U-turn up with a smile.

When a smile turns up,
You're nowhere to be frowned.

A smile is just a frown making a U-turn.

A smile is a mark on your face that helps you face up to making a mark on the world.

A smile is the best way to make your mark in the world.

A smile is a way for our lips to re-purse after rehearsing.

A smile lets our lips repurse until they get it up right.

Smiling is our body rehearsing for when we see God.

A smile is the best response to give.

A smile is the only thing that's okay to break into.

A smile says, "It's not your fault."

A smile is your brain on a break.

A smile is the best way for your lips to form an open mind.

A smile always fits your face perfectly.

A smile provides the best fit when you're having a fit.

A smile has no size, just sighs.

All smiles are different, but they have the same length: they all smile from ear to ear.

A smile is another way for our bodies to take a glee.

A smile is a way to make things more aglee-able.

Exercise your smile. It's all gain and no pain or sweat.

Exercise your right to smile.
It's all you have left to flex.

Every time you flex your smile, you do cheer-robics.

A smile is the shortest distance between two points of view.

A smile says, "I'm almost ready."

A smile is the beginning of something good.

You can't run out of smiles. They go on for smiles and smiles.

A frown is a depressed smile.

An upright smile gives you the best chance for not being turned down.

A smile lets you know you're okay.

A smile can melt the coldest heart.

Smiles let others know we're busy.

A smile is God's way of letting you sneak up on people.

Smiling is our God-given right.
Not smiling is downright frowned upon.

A smile is our face being a mime.

Smiles let us be mimes who say, "Be mine."

A world with smiles paints a grin portrait.

Smiles let our tongues rest.

A frown is a smile eraser.

I smile when my pants fit.

A smile is the calm before the scorn.

Seriously — it's not funny if you don't smile.

If we all committed a smile to the world, we'd be smiles ahead of our problems.

A smile is the way we communicate with giggle bites.

Even a small smile is a new big grinning.

A smile is a tee-smirk worn on your face.

A smile is under your nose because it knows it will lead to understanding.

A smile is the best seasoning for someone with good taste.

It suits a doctor to smile — less chance of lawsuits.

I smile thinking of sweet memories.

Many a smile has led one to sweet dreams that lead one to suite dreams.

Your smile says, "You're on the right path," and a smile keeps you on that path.

A smile is a pretty, bright idea.

Don't fail to smile. It might be the only bright idea in your life.

Notebook 3

A smile is your little love note to others.

I duly noted that a smile is your little love note to others. I noted how my Creator only asked me to do one thing in my life. He wanted me to tell others about Him and His good news. God is love and smiles are His little love notes reminding us of this one really important thing that He wants us to do. God wants you to make it your passion to know Him and tell others about Him. I see the word *passion* as a text telling me *i* do not want to *pass* on doing my passion and to do it before I pass on.

People usually have a passion for something. Hopefully it encompasses doing helpful things for people. Most people feel ordinary and don't feel like they've done anything that great. It comes down to our attitudes. We should be passionate about appreciating the power, gratitude, and wonder found in all the smaller things that we encounter. We don't appreciate the small yet valuable gems that glint and shine to glean our attention to what is most valuable in aiding us through our earthly lives.

We would have less problems if people were as good at doing things as they were about making excuses. The little things in life will refute all of our excuses and make us ashamed that we ever birthed them or shared them with others. A smile is a good example of a little thing that means so much. Don't tell me you can't smile or there's nothing to smile about. You can at least experience a smile on the faces of others who are all about you. Don't be great at making a great amount of excuses. Just excuse yourself with a smile.

A smile is an ease raiser without a rub.

God is perfect. He created a perfect smile so you would know you could reach perfection when you smile.

God does not use an eraser when he creates, but He did give a different rub to each smile that He created.

A calm smile is like a ripple that spreads over the calm surface of the water. It has the power to grow.

A smile is like an ambassador who is coming in peace.

A smile is your body's timepiece. It lets you know it's fun time.

A smile listens and conceals your tied tongue.

A smile is your spare ear and mouth to use when talking or listening.

A smile says, "I saw you take an extra one." You can give or take an extra smile with no problem.

God created a smile as *standard* equipment for every face, and your smile was built to be *automatic*.

The best way to chisel a person is to carve a smile on your face.

A smile reveals if your lips are lying or on the level.

A smile is formed by your lips lying correctly.

The best way to preview your smile is to let people have a view of a smile that's always there.

A smile extends from ear to ear. It's your communication line between your ears that reminds you to listen with a smile.

A frown is just a smile going down for a spell.

A smile says be a clown, be a clown, be a clown. A frown says, "I want to turn up and watch the clown."

A clown never frowns because, with a smile, the clown knows he or she will be smiles ahead when he or she acts up.

A smile is a preview of your coming attractions.

A smile is the period we apply between each sentence we utter.

Whatever you utter, it's an utter shame if you don't add a smile.

A criminal smiles after finishing each sentence.

You can construct the truest smile from lips that are lying all about and around us.

A smile is the finishing touch on the surface of your production.

A smile says, "You care to send the very jest."

A smile is hope because a smile says, "I hope to see you again." I hope to see you smile again.

A smile says, "Dear God, thank you for playing with me today."

It's not what you know, it's knowing when to smile and say no.

I smile when I get a seat on the aisle.

My smile is first class, in first class.

Your smile is dental floss for your mouth. It helps you to de-pick-ed the tooth.

A smile is the best gap to have between your teeth.

You can always wear a smile on your face. Just be more aware of it.

A smile says, "I'm the star of my own show."

You *win* when you *place* a smile to *show* off your face.

A smile can be one-dimensional. Two smiles are in the same plane. Three smiles speak volumes.

I always express a smile when I see an express line.

A smile is the body's express line where you can check things out.

I want to go with a smile on my face when I check out of this world.

A smile is an express line on your face that people check out.

I expressed a smile when my ex pressed my hand.

You will impress when you express a smile.

You can make your smile impressive just by pressing your lips when you're glad.

The world is as wide as your smile.

It's a small, smile world standing in a long line at Disneyland.

I smile when I see the word *smile* floating up on the milk while I'm enjoying a bowl of alphabet cereal.

I smiled when my bowl of alphabet soup spelled out soup.

You can smile away the time and never feel rushed.

Q: How many smiles does it take to change a lightbulb?
A: None. Bulbs aren't required for my smile to be bright enough to socket to you.

A bright smile serves to help lighten people's attitudes.

A smile is your attitude meter that reveals your personality when you meet her.

I smile when my plane is on time.

I smile when my plane lands safely.

A smile is the very best ad you can add to your face.

A smile on your face provides *U* with the power to adjust your attitude.

A smile gives you self mirth.

Smile every day and every day can become your mirth day.

A smile is mirth waiting for.

A smile is your source for staying the course.

A smile is mirth waiting to see you.

Your smile pre-sees you.

Your smile never ages, unless you haven't smiled in ages.

A smile is your mirth going forth to merge with other smiles.

You were born with a great smile. A smile is your place of mirth.

A smile is a good-looking dish's way of broadcasting.

It takes you turning your cheek for others to begin turning theirs.

A smile is one good turn that deserves another.

A smile is one good turn we need to turn others onto.

A smile is a mail slot for your face to receive the smiles others send your way.

A smile is a receiver in your face so you can attract others expressing their smiles.

A smile is *born* by being expressed out of your face.

I smile when deuces are wild. You can deduce that from my wild, wide smile.

A smile says you care about what others think, even if they don't care what you think.

Your smile is a stick to lean on when you're doing your shtick.

A smile on hand led to two in the bushes.

Smiles come in any length or size you width.

A smile is as natural as breathing one into your life.

Some people roam and some people stay home to pull down the shades so their skies are not cloudy all day.

A smile mirrors your image, so I imagine you'll smile more often.

A smile is an image in the mirror that dictates what you do with the rest of what you saw in the mirror.

Imagine that your smile reflects the exact same image on the face of our Heavenly Father.

A smile is your mirror that others can gaze into.

A smile does not have to be blinding to fuse to your face; it just has to be binding.

A smile is the best thing to make when someone says, "Make my day."

Your smile is a site for our eyes. Your smile is a sight for sore eyes.

A smile is our lighthouse flashing smiles across the surface of our face.

A smile is what lights up our eyes.

A smile occurs when the first perk of coffee appears to perk up my day.

A smile is a de-light, and not to be taken lightly.

A smile is like the sun: it always shines on those it touches.

The moon reflects the message that God's sun will be back soon.

A smile reflects the courage you've raised to face your fears.

The bigger the smile, the less room there is for trouble.

A smile helps you wipe the fear from your speech.

She wasn't pretty, but she had a pretty nice smile.

Having a smile is what can make your day, day in and day out.

A smile measures your potential, especially when it's electric.

Smile when you're tardy because it's never too late to show up with a smile.

A smile is the only thing that's always in style.

It's hard to smile when you're sick with pain, but a smile, no matter how painful, puts you on the road to recovering from your sickness.

Smiles are our lips giving thanks for your generous tips.

A smile is your lips checking out your façade.

When an expecting mom smiles, she molds the smile growing inside.

A smile gives your lips a chance to let loose and expose themselves.

Your smile can give you a better posture until you get back on your feet.

A smile is where you show your joy as coming from the fruit of your Spirit.

A smile lets us taste the fruit of God's Spirit within us.

A smile is a seal of God's promise that He lives in us.

Don't pray for God to just shine down on you. Pray that God's smile shines through and throughout you.

A smile is a great image to streak on a foggy mirror.

I smile when I see someone streaking.

A smile gets you over the mountains and through the valleys.

A smile that begins to cease is the surest way for a relationship to start to cease.

A smile says, "It's okay to accept defeat," but it's not a full surrender.

A smile says it's okay to accept defeat. Acceptance starts by emitting a smile that now says, "I lost this battle, but Jesus won the war."

If you want to be outstanding, try smiling while standing out in a crowd.

A smile is lip synching that's not fake or in need of practice.

A smile is the salt that keeps us from sweating in tight situations.

A smile is like salt that loses its flavor because it's useless if we act with dis-flavor.

A smile is like a seasoning you can use to look more tasteful when you don't like what you're tasting.

A smile is a palate cleanser so we speak in good taste.

A timely smile reminds people that it's time for them to smile back more often.

Smiles mirror your dreams.

It's not frowned upon to smile.

The first thing you should think of putting on in the morning is your smile.

A smile is the best way to show you're a good beau.

I can shave a smile right off your face with one sharp, cutting remark.

When we smile, we forget our needs and are more open to seeing the needs of others.

A smile is able to turn a beast into a lamb.

The best U-turn is when your two lips turn up to smile.

A smile is your valet-sparking service.

A smile is the only facial wrinkle that can shrink.

Smiles are the only wrinkles we want to see on our faces.

When you smile, it adds a new wrinkle to your personality.

A smile is a wrinkle that is pressed on your face.

An arresting smile helps you make bail.

Give a smile to help pick up that bale.

Use a smile as your armor for fending off amore.

His smile was arresting as he sat in his cell.

A smile should be arresting because it's a resting right smack on your face.

Her arresting smile led to her getting pinched.

There is no downside to a smile.

A smile is an impression on your face that helps you make a good impression on others. I'm always impressed when people return my smile.

I'm smiling in the rain because water can't melt me or my smile.

A smile says, "You care enough to bring your very best attitude."

A smile helps you get ahead when you smile and let someone go ahead of you in line.

Don't let your smile shrink when you talk to the psychiatrist.

A smile helps you choke back your swears.

A smile is a throttle that regulates how we say things, either softly to comfort or loudly to celebrate.

Smiles are monitors that help us watch our backs.

A smile is a censor for our lips.

A smile is God's lip balm to help us keep calm.

Smiling upward is the first step to calming down.

A smile is never far away. It's as close as you want it to glee.

I'm drawn to a smile because it's picture perfect.

A smile is not far away when you call to tell me you're near.

A smile says, "I live right around the corner."

It's easy to find your smile. Just take a turn at the ends of your lips.

A smile says, "I heard what you said," without actually having to disagree about what was said.

A smile helps you stick with it, so stick one on your face!

I smile when the weather is calm.

A smile forecasts a good outlook.

A smile lets you look out and see that your friends are looking out for you.

A smile is your lookout glower.

I smile when I'm back down from climbing up a mountain.

A smile asks, "What's on your mind?"

A smile traverses the many miles we travel in life.

A smile is a trail others are seeking.

A frown is an introverted smile.

You can smile anywhere you glow.

The lightest way to travel through life is to just pack a smile.

Your smile packs a punch. You won't get punched if you smile.

Your smile is about the only thing people shouldn't mind you having.

When you can't smile,
Eat some Snickers
Jest in the snick of time.

A smile is parked right on my face when ere I find a great parking space.

A smile is best shown when you're doing it on your own.

You can't see your smile without a mirror.
It's better to see it reflected on others.

A smile can be your measuring stick or shtick.

God owns your smile,
So you owe Him a smile
For smiling on you even when
You forget to smile back at Him.

We can only give talent, time, and money. It doesn't take much time or talent to smile, and once you do, you will see that a smile is priceless.

Your smile is unique and can't be replaced, and that makes it priceless.

The cost of a smile is what one is willing to play.

A smile is when your lips go out on a whim as you smile and go out for a swim.

Don't leave on a whim without remembering to take your smile.

A smile is like a car. It auto take you to where you want to go.

A smile is a headlight to guide your path.

You don't have to pack a smile to go on vacation. Your vacation is already planned to be full of smiles.

If you're going to pack a smile, you should use the one that's parked on your face when you're finished with packing and panicking.

A smile is your map that leads to buried pleasure.

A smile is a compass for your face to point you upward and onward.

Your mouth is your face mat upon which you place your smile.

A smile can give you goosebumps.
I don't smile when a goose bumps into me.
I smile when I get goosed.

You won't go out on a whim if you smile until the end.

When I eat snow, my smile turns into an ice giggle.

A smile causes frostbite when it's frozen on your face.

When you run out of smiles, there's more in the puntry.

I can't place your smile, but you can smile at my place.

A smile is a U Tube account telling your mouth tu-be smiling.

Frequent flyer smiles help with travel.

I'm a member of the smile high club.

The reservation clerk checked me out with a smile, but didn't notice me checking out her smile as she was too busy checking me in.

I take stock in my smile especially when my stock rises.

I smile when I'm nice and not naughty.

I smile when you're nice and naughty.

A smile is always yearning for more.

A smile is a glow that says go with the flow.

I never did see a smile I didn't like.

My smile left when you opened my door and it came right back when I closed it.

Your smile is like a car
When you make it a Beemer.

People will flip you a smile because you placed blueberry smiles on their pancakes.

The Homeland Security agent was very thorough. She even checked out my smile.

Airport guards always give me suspicious smiles.

A smile is like an awning that masks the shadiness on your façade.

I never did see a smile that I didn't like, especially when it likes looking back at me.

A smile says, "You can clap when you know you're happy."
I'm happy knowing I don't have the clap.

A smile is the embryo of a dream.

A smile is all weather when you smile whether you feel like it or not.

A smile on hand is worth two in the wishes.

Smiles result from the development of dreams.

A smile leads to the development of wishes kept to ourselves.

A smile expresses our desires.

We don't need instructions about how to smile; we just need to instruct people to smile.

You can smile without reading the instructions.

A smile is a conversation starter that ignites your speech.

A smile is a picture that's worth millions of words.

A smile can't trip you up if you don't put your foot in your mouth.

Raising a big smile is how your lips go surfing. Don't wipe them out.

A smile can do the wave when you can't stand.

God put a smile on the crest of a wave so you won't ocean it.

A smile says, "I'd like to stop and chat but I got to go."

Humming is a smile that's trying to sing.

A smile is self-wrought because it's self-taught.

If a picture is worth a thousand words, how come a picture of a beautiful smile leaves me speechless?

Smile and the world scrambles to figure out what you're up to.

A smile is self-fraught and needs not be taught. If a smile is too taut, your lips crack.

All you need to be taught to smile is to have a taut lip.

I smile when I'm riding my bike.

Smiling is like riding a bike: you never forget how to do it.

Everyone can afford a smile.
You can't afford not to smile.

Only a fool rushes in without a smile to places where only a wise person dares not go without one.

Don't ask why I smile. It's already so revealing.

A smile reveals that you want to revel in your life.

A smile is a revel without applause.

A smile is a great ambition, if your ambition is to smile regardless of your success.

A smile is the appetizer served before the main kiss from that dish.

A smile on hand led to two being held in the bushes.

Smiles are our irons so we can press our lips together.

A kiss is sealed with lips that lie together as they smile.

A smile opens your lips to greater possibilities.

A smile is a fortune teller. It says, "Maybe you're gonna get some."

A smile is your fortune teller. It says your smile is worth a fortune.

It's fortunate when you have an occasion to smile.

I don't need a break from work. I keep breaking a smile over the progress of my work.

You don't need to take a break if you just break a smile.

A smile is the silent light we beam on that Holy Silent Night.

A smile gives off light but not sound because it's meant to be seen and not heard.

A preponderance of smiles led to a smile-nt and a silent majority.

A smile says give me a break, when it breaks out all over your face.

A smile is a good way to egg you on without getting egg on your face.

A smile is your best sales tool.

A smile is the outer shell of your face that's okay to crack.

A smile is how you crack up under pressure.

A smile is like an egg because a smile is eggsactly what you should be hatching.

I don't kiss and tell, but I can tell you want a kiss. Just be glad I don't tell you who or what to kiss.

A smile is the best apparel to wear when things don't suit you.

Hatch a smile when you want to egg someone on.

A smile is like an egg: it's all white to be around yolks because a smile allows you to crack up. Just don't get any egg on your face.

A smile is like getting egg on your face: a smile appears on your face when you get a yolk.

When you get egg on your face, just tell them the yolks on you.

An entertainer knows a smile is a skill that says, "Go out and kill."

A smile is your most vital sign.

You can see smiles on people of either sex, especially when any of those people are having sex.

A smile makes you feel more secure by knowing no one can take it from you.

A smile secures me an easier passage when I'm waiting at the security checkpoint.

You can feel secure knowing God secured your smile permanently so it will last for eternity.

I smile knowing I have the Master's peace.

When you stir up a smile with love, you paint a masterpiece.

A smile is a God-given right that is exercised every time you smile right back at God.

You can't drown in your smile.
You can't smile while someone is drowning.
But you can smile that he or she didn't drown.

A smile helps pick you up when your vital signs are down.

A smile helps pass the time each time you pass the clock until quitting time.

A smile tells people you're pretty nice.

I have a pretty smile because I'm pretty fortunate I can smile at the cost of the care to maintain it.

One person's smile is another person's pleasure.

A smile is an air compressor that pumps up your chest.

A smile is a distraction that enables you to steal a kiss.

A smile is subject to change and availability.

A smile doesn't depend on the weather; it depends more on whether you're willing to give one.

A smile on your face tells you not to stand there but reach out and see it sitting on other faces.

A smile is a good standard to exhibit when you're in good standing.

A smile isn't wash and dry. A smile is more like watch and try.

A smile is so you can decorate your tree-mendous personality.

A smile makes you look important.

A smile is like the morning dew: do a smile every morning.
I smile when I drink Mountain Dew.

A smile is like a water drip. It appears when the drip stops.

A smile is like a river because it reminds you to smile and go with the flow.

A smile helps your flood of tears recede.

A smile is the best thing to get on someone's face.

When a smile is on your face, it's easier to deal with someone who's trying to get in your face.

A smile is the only thing that should be getting on your face.

A smile lets you come in first place when people know that you are placing their needs first in place of yours.

A smile puts you in first place when you first place one on your face.

A smile is like instant coffee: it perks you up the instant you smile.

I plant a smile on my face so people will dig me.

Face the world with a smile because a smile helps you face the world.

God put smiles on our faces to remind us that we're going to have to face up to Him.

God put smiles on our faces to give us tools that enable us to face the world by planting smiles on other faces.

When someone plants a smile on you, notice how yours crops up.

Planting smiles is how others crop up.

God gave us smiles so we can give it our best shots when our mouths start shooting off.

A smile is like a seed that you can plant knowing it can grow anywhere.

A smile may move others, but others may not help you move.

A smile is your FOR SALE sign that says you are ready to list-en.

A smile assures people your mouth is available for listening.

A smile is the same in every race, color, or creed.

My creed is to give a colorful smile to people of every race.

Smiles look the same on the faces of any race of people.

A cheesy smile lets you win the rat race by making people feel like they're not trapped.

A cheesy smile is a gouda thing.

A cheesy smile helps you bries through life.

A smile, properly cultivated, makes you seem more cultured.

A smile is like a seed that makes you less seedy looking.

A smile is like a seed that, when properly planted, gives you the best chance to succeed in seeing it grow on the faces you cultivated.

A smile can coerce others to do what you want.

A smile is God's answer every time we ask Him for a raise. God says, "Raising a smile could lead to a raise."

A smile is meant to get you to see that God is smiling even more and forever more on your life.

A smile helps us envision the sun on a cloudy day.

At daybreak and throughout the day, you should break into a smile.

Q: If you're caught smiling, do you have to pay a fine?
A: You don't have to pay when your smile is fine enough.

A smile pays for itself even when you give them all away to others.

A smile is the best way to give your face appeal that can't be peeled off.

A smile is your lips giving an open house to display your mood.

A smile can't go broke but you can go for broke and smile.

A smile will never leave you bankrupt. Others can give you theirs.

Giving with a smile on your face is better than giving the shirt off your back and not smiling.

A smile is still the *current see* that God gives to increase your face value.

A smile helps your appearance when you appear in court.

A smile is your Declaration of Independence.

God sends down a smile so we will look up to Him until things start looking up.

A smile gives us more time to judge others.

Smiles can erase our mistakes.

A smile can ease a wrong.

A smile acknowledges a joke.

A colorful smile shows people you're feeling in the pink.

A slice of any fruit can be cut to look like a smile; that's why it has such a peel.

A smile is my pause button so I can stop and think, *Hey, he's putting his paws on me!*

If you can't buy a smile, go where you can just start giving them and getting them freely.

Smiles are the best deposits we can make on our faces.

When you inject laughter, it raises a welt placed smile on your face.

A smile is better than Botox because it can smooth over wrinkles permanently.

The best way to raise kids is to raise a smile.

A smile says a wrong was righted.

A smile is a beam that helps you find your way back when you've been in pain.

A smile may produce a tug on the heart that says, "Your smile *beats* all others."

An amusement park merry-go-round produces an amazing smile parked right on your face.

A smile is an amusement park for your face.

Smiles abound when I'm found riding on the merry-go-round.

A smile is God's way to give a foretaste to us of His love until we see Him smile at us.

A smile is a pitch that makes you a hit because when you strike out you will look batter.

A smile is the best compliment we can pay ourselves.

A smile is a line you can give when you want to throw someone a curve.

God made us smile in the shape of a curve so we can strike out better when it's our turn to get battered. You had better strike out with a smile.

A smile says, "I'll succeed next time."

A smile might be one of the best gifts in life.

You have plenty of smiles to go around when you ride a merry-go-round.

It helps to put a smile in front of the nagging, so they don't see your tongue wagging.

A smile says you want to horse around.

I smile when I ride a horse, even if it's on a carousel.

I smiled because I was positive about my COVID test being negative.

Raising a smile is a way for your face to give itself a raise.

You can raise a smile even when your request for a raise is rejected.

A smile is a sign that shows you've been injected with laughter.

My smile tested positive and made me feel positive that I passed my test.

It's best to pony up a smile when you feel a little hoarse.

A smile is like a mushroom that turns me into a fungi.

If at first you don't succeed, just keep on smiling and look like a winner.

Don't rush a woman when she's dressing. You'll know she's ready when she smiles and then you can smile.

Get ready, get set, go smile.

A smile lets people know you're ready and set to glow.

You can have a ready smile even if you can't read.

A smile is the nicest look you could ever have.

When you didn't do your best, give them your best smile.

A smile is the nicest thing to see once you're out to sea.

A smile makes you appear more successful.

I smile when I hear I'm an heir.

A smile says, "I've got no-fault insurance."

A smile assures people that you acknowledge theirs.

A ready smile buys you time until you're ready to give an answer.

A smile is God's assurance that we're gonna be okay.

A smile is washable and watchable when you see it help a drip to try.

A smile is something we can give and receive at the same time.

You fawned over me with your smile. It's such a fond remembrance.

Giving a smile gets you what you want when what you want is to see it on others.

A ready smile will help you get ready for success.

If at first you don't succeed, keep on smiling until you do succeed.

Notebook 4

Your smile is a note without a quote.

Your smile is your note without a quote because when you smile, no words are needed; a smile says it all. However, that's not all I want to encourage you to do. If I am to accomplish my mission, I do not want you to miss the feedback from my readers on the power contained in their smiles. Most importantly, I do not want you to miss out on the importance of your smile.

We are all as unique as our smiles. We seem to have more differences than similarities, but we all have the potential to smile and appreciate how large a role a smile plays in conducting our voluntary actions.

My final desire is to share others' thoughts and words on the topic of smiles and smiling. I wrote about a few thousand of them, but I know there are untold more locked in the minds of my fellow human beings. Start thinking about your smile. Start writing down the thoughts you have about your smile. I know each will be unique and different from the ones in my book. Send them to me. I would love to hear what you come up with. If there is strength in numbers, then my mission is to increase people's awareness of the power of their smiles. I want to appreciate my smile, and my wish is that everyone gets to see and experience the power and importance of the human smile as well. Remember, we are the greatest of all God's creations. Humans posses the power and blessing of being able to give the greatest smiles.

She never masked her infectious smile.

A smile is a band of aid when you're alone and in pain.

A smile is your body's band-aid.

A smile is a band that turns up to aid you.

A smile is like a wide-band communicating device.

A smile is the real bond that ties us together.

A smile is contagious, but it's okay to pass it on.

A smile says, "Okay, in a little while."

I'm allergic to smiling. It makes me break out in laughter that's so bad I almost die laughing.

The cure for laughter is a bad comedy show.

If you're allergic to laughter, decrease and desist your smile's crease or you could end up deceased.

If you're allergic to laughter, then the anti-dote starts with you wiping that smile off your face.

A smile is shock therapy for your enemies.

A smile says, "Peace."

A smile is like a thank you to someone who's near to you.

A smile is your first aid kit.

A smile is your prying look that leaves you open to suggestion.

A smile is your wrench to keep others from bolting.

A smile is a circle that's halved enough.

A smile is a childproof cap to guard your lips.

Smiling isn't childish unless you're just kidding.

It's natural for children to smile. That's why we call them kids.

A smile is your body's power outlet. I get a charge out of your smile.

A smile is a recharged and recycled frown.

A smile is a recycled frown that wants to move up in life.

When you meet a grump, it's best to walk an extra smile with him or her.

You won't smile over others' blues once you walk a smile in their shoes.

I bought an app for smiling. It just said open and apply.

I looked up the instructions for smiling. They said it would apply to any *sure-face*.

A smile is an app your body uses for approval.

A smile might not prove a point, but it could get you ap-point-ed.

A smile is the current see when we ask for currency.

You can smile when you get a good buy, or you can smile when they say good-bye.

A smile is like money in the thank.

A broad smile makes you appear more well-rounded.

A smile is God's way to throw someone a curve.

A frown is a *sag jest ion* to smile.

A smile is the cheapest face-lift and mood enhancer.

A smile is a seal of God's approval.

A smile is God's approval that everyone can see.

A smile on your face is the best way to act like God.

A smile on your face helps you face each mile.

A smile can make you look pretty when you're petty.

A smile is God's finger on your lips.

A smile encourages you to keep looking in the mirror until your makeup makes you like how you look.

A smile is a cue you can view, when you don't have a clue.

A smile and a mouth are needed for you to get a pause port.

A smile lets you know the food is good.

A smile is as vital as food.

When a kid smiles, it's like food for *tot*.

I drink milk because it leaves a smile on my upper lip.

You can smile in any direction and find you're approaching perfection.

A smile gives you direction when you try to find your way. Compass the time with a smile.

A smile makes your face taut to show you've been taught to smile.

A frown is a smile that is just a drag.

It's not okay to act half bad because it's better to be good and show you half no bad.

Being half-bad is like an addict cutting his or her use in half, so now he or she does things half acid.

A smile is a nice pause to aid your cause.

A smile is sneerer to you than it sheens.

Sometimes her smile dims as she gets sneerer.

A smile is a sheen that is seen and not blurred.

When it comes to smiles, the greater the length the greater the strength.

A frown is a semi-circle that's getting sneerer to being a smile.

A smile is a great way to diet. Your smile says, "The pounds are melting."

A smile helps you scale your weighty goals.

Don't wait to be happy, just smile and be happy with your weight.

Used eyeglasses: second glances.

A smile will improve your chance of someone giving you a second glance at a second chance.

A smile is judged true when its content makes others content.

A smile is a sparking space for your mouth.

A smile is a noun without words. It's also a verb showing actions speak louder than words.

A smile says, "I tried."

A smile is for when your tongue is tied.

A smile is how you put your mouth on hold.

While eyes are staring, make sure your smile's not sneering.

I don't smile at erectile issues. A smile maintains the erectile tissues around your face.

Seventeen facial muscles are needed to smile. Don't let anyone muscle in on your smile.

God said, "Let there be smiles" and there were, and then He rested. When a smile rests on your face, no words are needed.

A smile right up front is God's way for you to let people know you're always right up front.

Seventeen muscles are used to smile.
Forty-three muscles are used to frown.
It's much easier to smile.

A colorful smile is like a rainbow that's seen all around.

A smile is like the part of the rainbow you can't see.

A smile is the gold fillings at the end of a rainbow of Skittles.

Staging a smile is the best way to upstage a frown.

A smile is what was lost when you were *frowned*.

I was bossed and now I'm *frowned*.

A smile is being frowned out.

A frown is only becoming if it's becoming a smile.

A smile is the best app to complete your *app-lick a tion*.

A smile is the freeze frame for your face.

Smiles are our faces winking at others.

You know you got it covered when a smile covers your face.

A smile says, "I got it covered."

A smile improves our *a-wear-nice*.

A smile is exercising our Bill of Rights.

A smile is easy to apply and is also a way for you to succeed when you try.

A smile presents another point of you to view.

Smiles decorate our faces, especially during the holidays.

A smile is the best decoration to complement someone being decorated.

A smile helps me find you in a crowd.

Models smile to reveal their *a-wear-nice*.

A smile expands the possibilities.

A smile helps the medicine go down.

Smiles are contagious because you break out in laughter.

Sometimes, all you can do is smile.

A smile says, "You have good taste."

Don't smile too much. You might end up disturbing the crease.

A smile signals your power is on.

My smile has total billing with no bills in my mail.

A smile is the sun shining on your two lips as you smile when the sun kisses your tulips.

You're the producer, director, and star of your smile, so start *acting* like you're smiling.

God is not *sneer* if you're not smiling. I sneerly missed seeing you smile.

A smile helps smooth miscues when you're not sure what you're viewing or doing.

A smile is never a play on words; it is a play we make without words.

A smile says, "Let's play."

A smile is your wave when you've got your hands full.

Smiles compliment our mouths whenever others compliment our smiles.

A smile is the best way to express our thanks to God for smiling on us with all His blessings.

A smile signals an answer to prayer.

If you don't pray, you don't have a prayer.

A caring smile provides for good childcare.

A smile is good adult care.

A smile says, "I do care."

A smile says, "Come over here."

A smile raises questions about why you're smiling.

A smile reminds me there's no place like home.

A smile is a good investment because it draws interest, and you can bank on it.

The more you smile, the more interest you seem to draw.

A smile is a masterpiece. It is a work of art lips.

A smile is a good expression for giving a good impression.

A smile is a great *open*-ing line.

God gave us smiles to let our lips create the Master's peace.

Q: What do you call putting your foot in your mouth?
A: A tiptoe through the two lips.

You can't put your foot in your mouth if you're smiling.

God is in a smile to give you more style.

A smile done well is your best silent welcome.

God is in a smile only when you are smile-in-g.

Amusement park hotel: The *Smile Inn*.

Your smile was made in God's image.

God sent Jesus to smile upon the earth.

God is in a mile when at it's end you see a smile.

A smile is the same in all languages, even sign language.

A smile gives texture to your lips so they can text-u're-okay.

Lips are our bodies' greenhouses. They keep our smiles growing.

A smile says, "I'm hip." A smile says, "I'll get over this broken hip."

A smile says, "I need you and you need to be smiling."

A smile helps me stay on my toes, doing great feats.

A smile is putting your best foot forward to accomplish that feat.

I smile when I'm needed. I smile even more when I'm kneaded.

A smile is the best way to keep your lips out of trouble.

When you smile, God's Holy Spirit always smiles back.

Draw a smile to show thou art picture perfect.

A smile is a nudge to end a grudge.

A smile is chicken soup for the chicken that's scared.

A smile art my way of showing thanks for being able to draw my next breath.

A *smile* is your *Return, Smile, Vould* you *Please* to God.

Your mouth is built to function like a PEZ dispenser that gives out smiles when you pop it open.

A smile is a silent giggle.

A smile ensures you keep a stiff upper lip.

A smile is best expressed with your tongue in cheek.

There's an art to smiling that draws out the best in others.

A smile is a pause so you can receive all the applause.

God put your lips in the center of your face so your smile can show you're well-balanced.

I've smiled in the past, and I've smiled at my past, but I can't get past not smiling.

A smile may be your only gift at the present moment.

A smile spans all generations of faces.

Don't pet sweaty things and don't sweat petty things.

A smile says, "Don't put me down and make me a frown."

Smiles matter more than most matters of fact.

Q: Why can't we just tattoo smiles on our faces?
A: It's so we can wipe that smirk off your face.

A smile says, "I didn't fart in the elevator."

A smile is a temporary tattoo tat fits you.

A smile says, "I'm gleed to see you."

A smile elevates my mood.

A smile is a tire jack because it's so uplifting.

A smile on an elevator is all you need to uplift others' spirits when they're going down.

A smile is a wise crack.

A wise crack can cause you to break out in a smile.

A smile is a facial etching that's fetching.

When a bright smile fades, it's called *pale-neon-tology*.

Try the smile diet; it's simple. Don't eat until a smile appears when you step on the scale.

I just ran off seven smiles while I was running my mouth off.

A frown is just the shadow of your smile.

You'll get a warm smile when the sun comes out after several days of rain.

A smile is a wile that can last for a while.

A smile opens doors because it's your thanks to those who open them.

Look for your smile's shadow. I know where it can be frowned.

A smile is a face magnet.

Launch a smile and don't lift it off.

A smile is like a rocket. It uplifts us to take the weight off our shoulders.

A smile is a way to gap-size your face.

A smile is the best way to christen every day.

A smile is God's gap-tism when you wet your lips.

A drool is a smile that's all wet.

A smile helps calm you during a duress rehearsal.

You can't lose your smile; it's right in front of your face.

A smile is your decal while you ride the bumper cars.

A smile is a spark that can set the heart on fire.

When you smile in the mirror, you can see God's angel smiling back at you.

A smiling face is the best way to face your day.

A frown may be a smile's reflection, but it is never a smile's direction.

A frown is meant to be a reflection, so you can turn it around with a smile.

A smile is just your U-turn to show off.

A frown is a smile headed in the wrong direction.

A smile is a frown that's been frowned out.

A smile is good when you tire because it pumps you up and inflates your spirit.

I smile more since I got to retire. Smiles never retire or get old. A smile says, "Until death do us part our lips."

A smile is the best rerun to watch.

A smile is an air purifier because it can help clear the air.

A smile is the most important part of a clown's costume.

The best thing to do with a frown is turn it into a smile.

Your smile is a gesture way of saying, "Hi!"

A smile is jesture laughing at a joke.

It's funny that the first thing people notice is your smile.

A smile says people can joke around with you.

A smile is made up of giggle bites.

A powerful smile shows you have the giggle-byte capacity.

I smile when I think Billy Cyrus should have named his daughter Smiley Cyrus.

The upside to a frown is a smile.

A smile persists when you don't get turned down.

Giggle-bytes lead to getting hooked on being caught up with her smile.

A smile never *disappoints* you.

Always keep your appointed time to smile.

I can't sing, but I can smile at your singing.

When you're down, get up with a smile.

Keep smiling, even if you think yours isn't beautiful. Just because birds can't sing beautifully doesn't stop them from singing.

A smile is your lips' purse so you can smile for a change.

We smile when we're embarrassed, but we should never be embarrassed to smile.

A smile is a good way to teach your kids how to deal with life.

A smile is the best way to do everything.

When you can't smile, make someone else smile by walking a smile in their blue shoes.

A smile says, "I have faith in you."

A smile is just a face adjustment for your attitude.

A smile is your best response to criticism.

A smile is just your face's way of telling you to lighten up by lighting up your smile.

A smile should be taken at face value.

You can always produce a smile; it's always on the tip of your lip.

A smile helps your body settle the tissue.
A smile helps you settle the issue.

A smile displays your best outlook on life.

Your best outlook on life is when you look out for a smile.

When I prepare s'mores, I notice s'more smiles appear and reappear as I prepare seconds.

A smile is your best glance to look good.

You'll improve your chances with smiling glances.

If I think, then I am. If I smile, then I think I am funny.

Smiling is just spamming while you're glamming.

Your smile spawned the thought that something was fishy.

Smile and you will be*grin* to see the answer.

It's a crime when a smile doesn't escape from your lips.

A smile is our being happy.

I smile when it's happy hour. But I smile more with our being happy and blessed each hour.

The word bless texts *b-less*. Be less of yourself and more of a servant to others and God will bless you by smiling down upon you.

A smile tells people you're blessed.

A smile is the key to open all the cells locked in that prison we call a body. A smile will free up your mind.

A smile helps you become somebody by making your body more becoming.

A smile is the key to freeing up and unlocking the answers found in your subconscious mind.

You're free to smile because smiles are free.

It's best to turn up a smile as you turn in at day's end.

A smile is a turn on. I never turn a smile down. It's frowned upon.

A smile is glitter you don't have to clean up.

You can smile freely, but I heard it pays to smile.

She was smiling when her face turned up.

I smile when I play in the snow because it's snow fun if you don't.

A smile is just flipping faces that house a smile.

I'm successful at flipping houses because I only sell to faces that house a smile.

People smile when things turn up. They smile even more when things turn out.

I smile when I get a good turn out to help with the turnip harvest.

Turn up with a smile.
It won't lead to a *down turn*.
Things will *turn out* and
You'll smile when you *turn in.*

Don't just sit there. Make sure a smile is sitting on your face.

A smile is a curve to show you how to deal with the curves life throws you.

If you smile when you dance, they won't notice you are stepping on their toes.

A smile helps you look more curvaceous.

A smile helps you take a turn for the worst and make it turn out better.

A smile says, "Get well soon."

They tell you to smile when they take your picture but not when they take an x-ray picture of your head.

A smile is an exclamation without sound.

It's nice to give your ex a smile as he or she ex-its.

Smiles have no sound, but it is a sound policy to always smile.

A smile measures how far you can grow.

A smile says, "Maybe you should be smiling."

They put a smiley face on dirty cars to provide a grin for the grime.

God made you in the image of His smile so He could share His with you for safekeeping until He returns.

Your smile is your treasure. Don't hide it on your chest.

Smiling is a talent you can perform in front of others.

You can't make up for lost time, but all is not lost if you take time to make up with a smile and a kiss.

A smile is a prelude to a kiss.

A smile is a pre-lube for a kiss.

A smile is a wish you could get a kiss.

Smiles are the best make-up for smoothing out the rough patches.

Your mouth comes with a smile proof chap.

A smile is God confirming He loves you.

I can't overdose on a smile, but her smile takes my breath away.

Q: How many people does it take to change a smile?
A: None. A smile never needs to change.

Maybe Frank Sinatra did it his way, but I did better. I did it smile way.

A smile is always on your lip if you're hip.

A smile is something to keep in mind.

You don't appreciate anything, even a smile, until it's gone. However, I would appreciate it if you would wipe that smile off your face.

On the seventh day, God rested and smiled, knowing He provided time for us to smile and rest.

Live out the rest of your time with plenty of time to rest and smile.

A smile is something we can share with others and still have enough to share with everybody we meet.

A smile says, "Happy Holidays!"

A smile can be your greatest present if you present a big enough smile.

Q: How many smiles does it take to change a lightbulb?
A: Just one. A smile is a de*light* and it never needs to be changed.

A smile shows you're living and not just existing.

The only riot I want to be at is the one where the entertainer is a riot.

Smiles may come and smiles may go, but my smile will come when my nurse comes so I can get my pain meds and I can go to the potty.

A smile is an idea dispenser.

An amicable divorce is when both file with a smile.

You can't divorce your smile, but you can smile when your divorce is final.

A smile lets you serve a summons to laugh.

A smile is a slice of life you don't cut out but splice in.

A smile is a sign that everything's fine.

A smile says we scored a touchdown, and we can keep playing.

Adults hardly ever smile. Kids smile all the time because they're laughing at what the adults are doing.

I smile during tea time. I smile when I get a tee time.

People play golf for enjoyment, but the only smile I see is from the cut on their golf balls.

When you smile you're never alone.

Your smile is the best reflection of you.

Smiles are the way we cover things *up* until they get the low *down* on us.

A smile says, "Cheers!"
A smile says, "You took my chairs."

A smile has your face for a cheer if a smile is sitting on it.

I stayed at a hospital called the Heal Inn.

Illusionists stay at the Mirage in Vegas.

Prophets stay at the Predict Inn.

Evel Knievel stayed at the Dare Inn.

Confused people stay at the Inn Decisive.

Optometrists stay at the View Inn.
Massage therapists stay at the Knead Inn.
Coaches stay at the Coax Inn.
Speakers stay at the Yell Inn.
Beggars stay at the Ask Inn.
Protesters stay at the Sit Inn.
Podiatrists stay at the Toe Inn
Smiles stay at the Grin Inn

Old age with all its challenges is just God messing with you until you get home.

Whenever I got in trouble as a kid, my mom would say sternly, "Wait until your father gets home." Now I smile because I'm a child of God waiting to get to my Father's home.

Overeating rich, fatty food will only lead you to an early gravy.

If you smile with red lipstick on, you get to part the Red Glee.

A comedy club is a Smile Inn.

I smile at the offhanded remarks that I face in life.

A smile is like giving your face a hand.

A smile is simply a big thank view.

A smile is a feast for the eyes and the ayes and the aye, aye, ayes.

The best way to maintain a smile is to constantly use it.

The quickest thing you can do to improve your appearance is to turn your cheeks up to smile.

A smile is God cheeking up on you.

As a writer, I've always looked for someone or something to inspire me. Now I'm at the age where I'm just writing as my revenge.

A smile forms when I'm done with the long list of forms.

You can smile and give your all even if all you gave was a smile.

If you can't smile when you do something, then don't bother.

A smile is your very own "special occasion." Celebrate it openly more than just occasionally.

If all you can give is a smile, give 'em your best smile.

A smile is your special occasion to look good.

A smile on your face says your smiles ahead.

Maximum security at the state penitentiary was so tight not even a smile broke out.

The warden was so proud of his perfect record of no escapes that a smile finally broke out on his face.

A smile should break out whenever anyone retires.

A smile is meant to be taken as all you can meet.

A smile is just your lips concealing a yawn.

A smile is just your lips extending a playcation.

The best way to tune up your face is with a smile.

When life slaps you in the face, don't turn the other cheek. It's better to turn up both cheeks and smile at some slapstick comedy.

A smile is the best revenge.

He who laughs last is the one who has a smile that lasts.

The best thing to turn up is a smile. It's telling you that things will turn up.

A smile says, "You're welcome."

A smile should always be out when you come in.

Stop and smile anywhere you go.

Your smile stays up when your fever is down.

A frown is a smile that's just recalculating.

When you're right, a smile is all that's left.

When you do things right away, I'm left with a smile.

It's not hard to smile when it helps to soften the blow.

You can speak softly and carry a big shtick by smiling.

You can speak loudly with a soft smile.

A smile speaks louder than words.

A smile speaks smiles about you.

They smile in your face, all the time they want to take your place — the smack dabbers.

If you want to take someone's place, take a smile over to his or her place.

When they smile in your face, face them with a smile.

A smile is your baton to help you face the music and conduct yourself properly.

I bask in a big smile, eating my favorite ice cream at Bask-in Robbins.

A smile springs to my face when I see the first robin of spring.

A smile is a basket you carry in case you happen to turn into a basket case.

A smile is good for any moment when you just take a moment to realize that it only takes a moment to smile.

A smile is just a moment of merriment.

A smile is simply your face's door opener. Make it automatic.

A smile is your face's transmission to help keep you rolling along.

A smile is just your face using Uber. A smile will take you places.

A smile can greet on Trick or Treat night.

A smile says, "That's what I think of what you been thinking."

Your smile is the best way to say thank you right to your face.

Your smile is how you fix things.

A smile is like a developer that pictures the solution to your problem.

A smile is your face entertaining your smiling guests.

A smile is the only entertainment some faces ever get.

The best way to entertain is to entertain a smile.

When someone smiles back, it's like having instant replay on FaceTime.

I smiled when he said he would go. I smiled even more when he came back with food.

A smile is FaceTime for your ego.

Smiling is an instinct that only stinks when you hold your smile in.

A smile keeps them guessing as to who farted in the elevator.

A smile is your elevator to face the ups and downs of life by elevating your mood.

A smile is your Medal of Honor to honor any occasion you meddle in.

A smile is a declaration declaring your face value.

A smile is God presenting your face with His decoration to honor you.

A smile pleases God because He sees you're using His gift to you.

A smile is a glance hoping for a chance.

I shore see a smile when I'm on the seashore.

A smile is a gift only if you reveal it.

You can revel in a smile even when you're reviled.

God sees you when you're smiling.
He sees when you're awake.
He even sees you when your smile is just a fake.

God gave us smiles to help us through our trials.

You can't lose with a smile knowing God's on your side smiling.

God gave us smiles to share as His way of showing people how much He cares.

God gave us smiles so we won't be frowned out.

A smile is for when you care to give the very jest.

A smile is always there for the basking.

A smile rises when my stocks are rising.

A smile is taking stock in yourself.

A smile is the best stock to market. It always pays dividends.

A smile is the best thing to multi-task.

A smile lets you multi-bask.

Always give a smile even before they ask.

Your smile will last longer if your lights don't short out.

A picture of you smiling will last longer if you don't develop the negative.

A smile is God's built in GPS that directs you to delight in Him.

When all is lost, all you have to remember is not to lose your smile.

A smile is just your face's way of giving itself a face-lift.

Don't get cross or angry. Just put a smile across your face.

God gave us smiles so we could have at least one thing everyone could do right.

The best way to be right is to smile right away.

Paint a smile on your face and you're less likely to get the brush off.

A smile is art from our Father who art in heaven.

A smile is God's heart showing He-art.

A smile is God's artwork drawing us to picture Him always.

Always apply a smile with love. It shows you love to smile.

A smile is your heartfelt way to show how your heart feels.

A smile is what surfaces from deep in our hearts.

A smile is the best heart monitor to place on your face.

Even a small smile can make a big difference.

God planted a smile on your face so you could grow up.

A smile is the best way for you to glow up.

A smile helps keep this clump of dust from becoming dust gusting.

Smiling is a gesture way to thank God.

A smile exhibits who you art.

A smile is a band-aid we can apply when we're hurt.

A smile with kindness shows the kind of person you really are.

A smile depicts that you want them to pick you.

A smile helps you when you're feeling frown.

A smile is God's clothing that best suits you.

A smile is your key to open a person's heart.

A smile is the door that opens the hearts of those who would knock you.

A smile is the key that God gave you to open up a relationship with Him.

A smile is how your face cracks up when you hear something funny.

A smile is your billboard that says attractions are coming.

A frown is just a coming retraction.

Your smile is very attractive. Keep it active.

When you visit others, a smile is your best coming attraction.

I was in line to get some punch at a comedy club called the Punch Line.

When you hear the punch line, a smile is what's lining your lips.

A smile is the way your face puts on a comedy show.

A smile is just your comedy showing.

A comedian smiles when it's standing room only. I can't stand you always smiling at me.

Smile when your slip is showing. It'll help you skirt the issue.

Smile. Your smile is showing.

A smile is your call to the riled.

A smile is your face stressing all your good points.

A smile is laughing at yourself.

A smile is an extension of your personality.

A smile is a human face extension.

I see an extended smile on your face as you enjoy getting hair extensions.

God gave smiles so we can express our greatest talents.

You may not have talent, but you can have a talented smile.

A smile is the extension where your face can be reached or breached.

A smile is an etching you can start from scratch.

A smile is your phone extension whenever you extend it to call on others.

If you don't cramp your smile,
You won't cramp your style.

A smile is best used when you're face to face with any situation.

Face it — my smile cracks me up.

A smile is like your phone extension, so don't give a phony smile.

A smile is your body's pleasure meter, so go ahead and mete out your pleasure.

The best way to meet is with a smile.

When two smiles meet, they become won.

A smile spreads more easily when it's warmer.

A smile is so you can inject laughter. Smile and give it a shot.

I smile when an injection didn't hurt.

It doesn't hurt to smile because a smile is soothing.

A smile is your first aid for maintaining a healthy relationship.

It doesn't hurt to smile. A smile helps you to get over your hurt-les.

God gave us smiles to help when we're shy. God said, our smiles say it all.

A smile is the gate guarding your heart.

Put a smile on your face; it's a great way and a gate way to meet others and open new doors.

Smile at all costs because it costs nothing to smile.

A smile is a crease that is meant to in*crease.*

I told my boss I need a raise,
But all he did was raise a smile.

A smile says, "Okay, spread out."

When a smile breaks out after you break your bone, it's a sign that the healing's begun.

A smile reveals a lot about who's making it.

A smile is a special delivery from your face.

I'm smiling after having a good breakfast.

I smile after I break a fast.

A smile is a gift that you don't need to wrap or rap.

Don't wrap a smile; it's only meant to enrapture you.

An ounce of smile is mirth more than a pound of slur.

A smile says, "I made it" by making sure I smiled.

A smile is your own personal signal to others.

A smile signals I'm single.

A single smile can light up the world.

A smile is a good point at which to make up.

A smile is a Valentine you can send to a heart.

When you're all wrapped up at work, you can wrap a smile around your face to show that you're gifted at doing your job.

A smile is mirth giving.

An explosive smile let's your face have a launch break.

When I get up, I'm fast to break a smile even before I have breakfast.

A smile is God's finished work on our temples.

Flash your smile when you're in a flash flood.

A smile flooded her face when her house wasn't flooded.

Got smile? Don't leave or go home without it.

I smile on my return to my home sweet home.

A smile is your credit card that keeps you from being declined.

A smile is your face streaking.

Your intentions are bared when a smile streaks across your face.

I smile when someone sneezes because a smile says, "I'm looking achoo."

A smile is just your face rolling out the red carpet.

A sure face is one with a smile on its surface.

A smile is mirth waiting for fun to start.

A big smile is a breadth of fresh air.

A big smile is the *bread*th of life.

A smile is an expression that expresses you want to have fun.

A smile is just a robe for your face while you're performing ae*robe*ics.

A smile makes you the strong, silent type of person I want to hang with.

Hang a smile on your face and people will want to hang around your place.

A person of few words doesn't have to serve any sentences.

A smile is the best way to finish a sentence.

I smiled when I completed my prison sentence.

A smile doesn't need words, because sometimes it may leave you speechless.

A smile is your Master's peace, made for His masterpiece.

A smile is all that's needed to become a person of few words.

A smile cannot lie unless it's lying on your face.

A drink *an-a-log* on the fire makes me smile.
A smile is a big *dig-it-all* display.

You can go on a mile a minute just as long as you smile each minute.

You don't want to be over the smile limit on the expressway. It's your ticket to a messed demeanor.

Apparently, a smile appears to make people better parents.

A smile in time produces nine.

I smile because I'm smitten by my kitten.

A smile is like a party decoration hanging on my face.

A smile is your mouth riding back and forth on a swing.

I like to relax and smile whenever I'm on a porch swing.

I smile when they deliver my new Porsche.

Your smile is there for your face to have a party.

Parting with a smile is the best way for people to part.

A smile is Snapchap for your face.

Keeping a smile glued to your face will let people know you're not stuck up.

A smile plays a big part whenever people are apart.

I smile when I swear to tell the truth without using any swear words.

I smile seeing you polish off that big Polish dog.

Smile like you mean it, as we were meant to smile.

Wise men glow where only fools rush grin.

A smile is your lips clapping because they're not chapping.

A smile says you don't have to watch pout.

> Smile — this is the end. However, a smile
> will never end, because it goes on for smiles
> and smiles to grin-finity and beyond.

About the Author

Now retired, Dr. William J. Kalanta was a podiatrist for over forty-five years. For a long time, he wanted to be a comedian and play to standing room only crowds. Then it hit him: a podiatrist and comedian are alike and do the same thing. They're both just pulling your leg. He now writes comedy books with lots of jokes about feet and all the funny aspects of life.

Made in the USA
Middletown, DE
02 July 2023

34456869R00097